UNDERSTANDING FINANCIAL STATEMENTS

A Guide for
Non-Financial Readers

James O. Gill

CRISP PUBLICATIONS, INC.
Los Altos, California

UNDERSTANDING FINANCIAL STATEMENTS
A Guide for Non-Financial Readers

James O. Gill

CREDITS
Editor: **Michael G. Crisp**
Designer: **Carol Harris**
Typesetting: **Interface Studio**
Cover Design: **Carol Harris**
Artwork: **Ralph Mapson**

The cartoon on the cover has been reprinted by permission of the author Sidney Harris and is from the book, "WHAT'S SO FUNNY ABOUT BUSINESS?", ©1986 William Kaufmann, Inc., 1990 Crisp Publications, Inc., 95 First Street, Los Altos, CA 94022.

Crisp books are distributed in Canada by Reid Publishing, Ltd., P.O. Box 7267, Oakville, Ontario, Canada L6J 6L6.

In Australia by Career Builders, P.O. Box 1051, Springwood, Brisbane, Queensland, Australia 4127.

And in New Zealand by Career Builders, P.O. Box 571, Manurewa, New Zealand.

Library of Congress Catalog Card Number 89-81248
Gill, James O.
Understanding Financial Statements
ISBN 1-56052-022-1

INTRODUCTION

This book was written for those not familiar with basic financial analysis. Its purpose is to explain fundamental concepts in a clear and understandable way and to provide simple tools that can help readers apply what has been learned to their business needs or interests.

UNDERSTANDING FINANCIAL STATEMENTS is not highly technical. It is also *not* a complete text on financial analysis. There are several excellent books that provide more sophisticated analytical techniques. Because of its simplicity, several liberties were taken with ''pure'' financial definitions to achieve clarity. However all definitions are basically correct. If you choose to delve further into financial analysis you will learn that there are several variations of accounting methods that will provide fine tuning to the basic concepts you obtain from this book.

The material presented in the following pages while not complex, but will take some time to master. It is suggested that you first skim through the book to obtain an overview of the material and then start again from the beginning. Going step-by-step and using the blank forms to work up your own ratios and percentages will give you a level of comfort. By the time you have completed this book, you should have achieved control techniques that will work in your business.

Good luck!

James O. Gill

i

ADDITIONAL WAYS TO USE THIS BOOK

UNDERSTANDING FINANCIAL STATEMENTS (and the other self-improvement books listed in the back of this book) can be used effectively in a number of ways. Here are some possibilities:

Individual Study. Because the book is self-instructional, all that is needed is a quiet place, some time and a pencil. By completing the activities and exercise, a person should not only receive valuable feedback, but also practical ideas about steps for self-improvement.

Workshops and Seminars. The book is ideal for pre-assigned reading prior to a workshop or seminar. With the basics in hand, the quality of the participation should improve. More time can be spent on concept extensions and applications during the program. The book can also be effective when a trainer distributes it at the beginning of a session, and leads participants through the contents.

Remote Location Training. Copies can be sent to those not able to attend ''home office'' training sessions.

Informal Study Groups. Thanks to the format, brevity and los cost, this book is ideal for ''brown-bag'' or other informal group sessions.

There are other possibilities that depend on the objectives, program or ideas or the user. One thing for sure, even after it has been read, this book will serve as excellent reference material which can be easily reviewed.

TABLE OF CONTENTS

(continued next page)

Understanding Financial Statements

TABLE OF CONTENTS (Continued)

ABOUT THIS BOOK

This book is written not only for new business owners or operators, but also for those who want better control over the business they manage.

During financial seminars, small business managers regularly mention their frustrations in ''getting a handle on the financial side of their business.'' These individuals have often been successful establishing a business, but have been searching for financial tools that enable them to take charge. A business is often described in anatomical terms: management is the brain, marketing is the muscle, and finance is the blood. Without the financial aspects (such as a flow of cash) the brain becomes uncommunicative and the muscle unresponsive. Understanding the basics of finance (including the proper control of cash), is essential if any business is to survive and succeed.

Starting a business requires an idea, some self confidence, and some initial funding. Not much more. Staying in business (i.e. becoming successful) requires financial management. For example, it is essential to know how to interpret a balance sheet and profit and loss statement. These financial tools tell you how to control your business and make it perform the way you expect.

Over half of all new businesses (excluding franchises), fail within four years. Another 30 percent don't last 10 years. Many of the survivors stay alive, but stagnate without reaching their full potential. Often, a lack of capital is cited as the reason a business failed. This reason is often true of potentially successful businesses that have no trouble obtaining customers. Ironically, quick but uncontrolled success has caused the downfall of thousands of businesses because owners or managers were unaware of the financial reasons behind their success and blindly over-expanded.

The financial information and techniques presented in this book can help a small business person understand *what* is happening, *why* it is happening, *what* to do, and *when* to do it to make things happen the way you want them to happen.

ABOUT THIS BOOK (Continued)

You will cover basic strategies and simple analytical tools that can help you:

1. Discover what your business is doing compared to similar businesses.
2. Determine financially whether you are making progress each quarter or year and understand why.
3. Develop a financial plan for the future.

This book is a reference manual. There is no need to memorize the contents. More emphasis should be placed on thinking about your business as you develop and compare ratios. The page-by-page layout of ratios (and other tools) will enable you to refer to those that are significant to your business at the time you want to use them. Not all of the ratios and techniques were meant to be used every time you check the health of your business or determine a future strategy, but you should be aware of those most applicable to your situation.

You will be introduced to eleven standard ratios. As a general rule, several will be meaningful once a month, others will be important once a year. Still others will be useful as your business grows. These ratios are for you to apply when they are right for you. There is no hard and fast rule when to use ratios, they are simply tools that can help you succeed.

IT IS GOOD BUSINESS TO UNDERSTAND BASIC FINANCE

WHAT THIS BOOK CONTAINS

This book will help you learn to:

★ Understand and evaluate the role of finance in your business.

★ Recognize the difference between cash and profit.

★ Know when borrowing makes sense and provide tips about dealing with your bank.

★ Understand what a balance sheet and profit and loss statement *really* show.

★ Know where to obtain data that is meaningful for your business.

★ Compare your organization with your competitors or industry.

★ Predict the future from past trends.

★ Get more productivity from your organization's expenses.

★ Understand basic financial terms when you read about them or hear others use them.

It is important for any business owner, new or old, to understand where the business is making money and where it is not. This is the function of finance. By knowing the fundamentals of business finance you can make more money during good times and lose less during bad periods through proper planning and informal decision making.

GOALS AHEAD

GOALS

The goals of this book are to:

1. Describe how balance sheets and profit and loss statements are prepared and what each means to a business.

2. Introduce simple ratios and proportions and show how easily they are developed and used to derive more meaning from a balance sheet and profit and loss statement.

3. Explain how to examine expenses and furnish proven ways to help you get better productivity from your expenses.

4. Provide four tested techniques that will enable you to exercise better control over your business finances.

This book is designed to help you meet the above goals by taking you through the following six steps:

| STEP 1 | To learn how the two main financial statements of any business, (balance sheet and P&L) are prepared and used. |

| STEP 2 | To introduce ratios and proportions and shown how easily they are developed and used. |

| STEP 3 | To explain different ratios and then provide examples that show how to get more meaning from your balance sheet and profit and loss statement. |

| STEP 4 | To teach how to perform a ratio analysis. During this step you will learn how to collect data and compare your ratios with those of competitors. |

| STEP 5 | To understand how to logically examine expenses. This is important because if price or sales volume can't be raised, lowering expenses may be the answer to success or survival. |

| STEP 6 | To learn four proven methods to control your business, (i.e. projecting how much cash you will need, when you need it, having enough cash for expansion, a new product introduction, or a sale). |

UNDERSTANDING FINANCIAL STATEMENTS will teach some fundamentals, but will not make you an expert. It will help to clear up some misunderstandings about finance but will not make you a CPA. It simply gives you some tools that will help you control and predict the future of your business.

PART 1

LEARNING THE BASICS

MINIMUM COMPETENCY: LEARNING THE BASICS

It is a demonstrable fact that stagnation or failure of a business often comes from over-buying, over-trading, or over-expanding. For example, a lumber yard significantly increased sales for three straight years then failed. Why? Because the owner couldn't resist a bargain. He over-bought too much of too many items that were offered with volume discounts. He used up so much cash that his on-going expenses, such as rent, utilities and salaries couldn't be paid on time. Similarly, a plastics manufacturer had a modern, labor-saving plant; well-stocked inventory, and increasing sales. But this same manufacturer had to let go of some ownership because a current loan couldn't be paid. Why? Because sales were obtained by offering loose credit terms and discounts. The results were that no cash was available to pay current debts. Another new company developed a new product that quickly became sought-after. It was so much in demand that the company borrowed heavily to build a new plant and production line. It accepted more orders than could be reasonably fulfilled in the required time frame and ended up delivering products very late. By the time the new plant was ready, demand had diminished and many of the old orders were cancelled. Unfortunately the debt was not. What happened? The business was sold to pay the debt. The business had over-expanded because it did not do a good job of financial analysis.

The difference between failure and success is *not* always the **lack of product knowledge** or of **failing to put in long hours.** More often it is not understanding the financial situation. Because new businesses usually have financial reports such as a balance sheet and a profit and loss statement prepared by someone in the family or by a CPA, owners or managers often do not understand the financial implications and make poor choices.

To achieve a minimum competency in finance it is essential to thoroughly understand balance sheets and profit and loss statements. This is what you will read next.

THE BALANCE SHEET

THE ANATOMY OF A BALANCE SHEET

The typical balance sheet displays the business' assets on the left side of the page and liabilities and net worth on the right side like this:

BALANCE SHEET	
ASSETS =	LIABILITIES + NET WORTH

Assets are normally broken into two main categories: current assets and fixed assets. Current assets usually mean anything that can be converted to cash within one year. Fixed assets are more permanent items like buildings or major equipment.

Liabilities are similarly divided. They are normally shown as current liabilities (that which is owed with one year) and long term debt. Current liabilities include bills for items such as inventory, salaries, rent, etc. Debt is normally items that by agreement need not be paid back quickly, such as a mortgage or long-term note.

The **difference** between assets and liabilities equals net worth. That is, after all bills and notes are paid, anything left is called net worth. Another definition is that net worth is what is due the owner(s) of the business once all liabilities have been paid.

$$ASSETS - LIABILITIES = NET WORTH$$

OR

$$ASSETS = LIABILITIES + NET WORTH$$

Why Is It Called A "Balance Sheet"?

The key word is *balance.* Because both the total assets and the liabilities and net worth totals are the same, they balance. This is true even if liabilities exceed the assets. In this case, net worth becomes negative and it must be subtracted from the liabilities, instead of being added.

HOW A BALANCE SHEET IS PREPARED

A balance sheet is a document that uses the principle of double entry accounting. It is called double entry, because each business action affects two or more accounts. For example a sale will increase cash or accounts receivable but decrease inventory. An account can be cash, inventory, money you owe (accounts payable), or owed to you (accounts receivable) etc. Accounts are organized in categories called current or fixed assets on one side of the sheet, and current or long-term liabilities on the other. Assets and liabilities (plus net worth) must always balance (hence the name "balance sheet"). A complete glossary of basic terms is provided on page 12 for easy reference.

Let's suppose that a new business was started with the owner's savings of $100,000. The beginning balance sheet would look something like this:

ASSETS	LIABILITIES
CURRENT ASSETS	NET WORTH
Cash $100,000	$100,000

The owner then decides to stock her store, and purchases $50,000 of merchandise *(Inventory)*, but pays only $25,000 in cash (this will reduce *Cash* by $25,000) and promises to pay the other $25,000 in thirty days, (this creates a new account called *Accounts Payable*) which is placed under the category of *Current Liabilities.*

The Assets balance sheet would now look like this:

ASSETS		LIABILITIES	
CURRENT ASSETS		**CURRENT LIABILITIES**	
Cash	$ 75,000	**Accounts payable**	**$ 25,000**
Inventory	**$ 50,000**	NET WORTH	$100,000
TOTAL	$125,000	TOTAL	$125,000

The balance sheet is in balance with the addition of $25,000 that is owed to the vendor. It is placed under current liabilities because it is due to be paid back in a specified period of time which is less than one year. Current assets are those items that can be converted into cash within a year.

HOW A BALANCE SHEET IS PREPARED (Continued)

Now let's suppose that the owner buys a building for $100,000. She puts $25,000 down and obtains a $75,000 mortgage for the remainder.

The balance sheet would now look like this: *(Note the addition of two new accounts, one called long-term debt, because it is to be paid over a period of longer than a year; and the second account called fixed assets which includes land, buildings and equipment).*

BALANCE SHEET			
CURRENT ASSETS		**CURRENT LIABILITIES**	
Cash	$ 50,000	Accounts payable $ 25,000	
Inventory	$ 50,000	TOTAL CURRENT LIABILITIES	$ 25,000
TOTAL CURRENT ASSETS	$100,000	**LONG TERM DEBT**	
		Mortgage	**$ 75,000**
		TOTAL LONG TERM DEBT	$ 75,000
FIXED ASSETS		NET WORTH	$100,000
Building	**$100,000**		
TOTAL FIXED ASSETS	$100,000		
TOTAL	$200,000	TOTAL	$200,000

THE BALANCE SHEET (Continued)

When sales are made inventory will decrease and cash will increase. If some sales are made on credit, a new account called ACCOUNTS RECEIVABLE WILL NEED TO BE ADDED UNDER CURRENT ASSETS. Let's suppose that $20,000 of inventory is sold for $25,000, ($15,000 is received cash and $10,000 is on credit).

The balance sheet would look like this:

BALANCE SHEET XXX COMPANY YEAR END 19XX			
ASSETS		**LIABILITIES**	
CURRENT ASSETS		CURRENT LIABILITIES	
Cash	**$ 65,000**	Accounts payable	$ 25,000
Accounts receivable	**$ 10,000**		
Inventory	**$ 30,000**	TOTAL CURRENT LIABILITIES	$ 25,000
TOTAL CURRENT ASSETS	$100,000	**LONG TERM DEBT**	
		Mortgage	**$ 75,000**
		TOTAL LONG TERM DEBT	$ 75,000
FIXED ASSETS		NET WORTH BEGINNING	$100,000
Building	$100,000	GROSS PROFIT*	5,000
TOTAL FIXED ASSETS	$100,000	NET WORTH ENDING	105,000
TOTAL	$205,000	TOTAL	$205,000

(*profit from example sale)

Note that this business action affected three accounts which are on the asset side of the balance sheet, one account (INVENTORY) lowered, the CASH ACCOUNT INCREASED AND A NEW ACCOUNT CALLED ACCOUNTS RECEIVABLE WAS ADDED, so that the total did not change.

To complete the balance sheet the company name and address has been added along with the date of preparation. The balance sheet is a snapshot of how a business stands *at any given point in time.*

Now let's see how the profit and loss statement is prepared.

THE ANATOMY OF A PROFIT AND LOSS STATEMENT

The profit and loss statement shows the total actions of a business over a **period of time** be it a month, a quarter or a year.

The profit and loss statement, or P & L, is sometimes called an income statement. It begins when a sale is made. So the *first entry* or account would be *sales*. This is how the $25,000 in sales would look on the profit and loss statement.

Sales	$25,000

The next entry would be *cost of those goods sold*. Let's say that the cost of goods sold was $20,000. Cost of goods normally is the manufacturing cost, freight from the supplier, royalties, etc. Cost of goods is subtracted from sales to show a *gross profit* of $5,000 (gross profit is the money left over before deducting expenses and federal taxes).

The added entries would appear on the profit and loss statement as shown below:

Sales	$25,000
Cost of Goods Sold	$20,000
Gross Profit	$ 5,000

The next entries that go on a profit and loss statement are the expenses connected with running a business. Expenses are either cash or accrued. In the example below, expenses totalling $1640 are identified.

The profit and loss statement would now look like this: (Note that it has a heading and that it covers a **period of time,** in this case one month).

PROFIT AND LOSS STATEMENT
XXX COMPANY
JANUARY 1 THROUGH JANUARY 31 19XX

Sales		$25,000
Cost of Goods Sold		$20,000
Gross Profit		$ 5,000
EXPENSES:		
Owners Wages	$500	
Salaries	900	
Delivery	50	
Bad Debt	20	
Insurance	30	
Taxes (local)	10	
Interest	50	
Advertising	80	
Total expenses		$ 1,640
	NET PROFIT (before federal taxes)	$3,360

(The total expenses are subtracted from the gross profit to give net profit before federal taxes of $3,360.)

GLOSSARY OF BALANCE SHEET TERMS

The balance sheet that will be used as an example for the remainder of this book is shown on the facing page. Following are definitions of the terms used in the balance sheet.

ASSETS — The cash, money owed, merchandise, land, buildings, and equipment that a company owns or that has money value.

CURRENT ASSETS — The sum of cash, notes, and accounts receivable (less reserves for bad debts), advances on inventories, inventories, and any other item that can be converted into cash in a short time, usually less than a year.

CASH — Money you have control of and access to.

ACCOUNTS RECEIVABLE — The monies owed to the company for merchandise, products, or services sold or performed but not yet collected.

INVENTORY — For a manufacturing firm it is the sum of finished merchandise on hand, raw material, and material in process. For retailer and wholesalers, it is the stock of salable goods on hand.

FIXED ASSETS — Land, buildings, building equipment, fixtures, machinery, tools, furniture, office devices, patterns, drawings, less salvage value and depreciation.

LIABILITIES — Everything that a company owes to a creditor; liabilities are the debts owed by the company to others. Liabilities are accounts such as: notes payable, accounts payable, or accruals. There are two categories of liabilities, current liabilities and long term liabilities, or as used in this book, long term debt.

CURRENT LIABILITIES — The total of all monies owed by the company that will fall due within one year.

NOTES PAYABLE — Money borrowed by the company that will be paid back within one year.

ACCOUNTS PAYABLE — Sometimes called trade payables, these are the total of all monies owed by the company to a supplier or vendor for raw material or products or merchandise that is to be used to make goods for sale or to be resold as it was received.

ACCRUALS — Taxes or wages that are accumulated against current profits but not yet due to be paid.

LONG TERM DEBT — Sometimes called long term liabilities, it is all the obligations such as mortgages, bonds, term loans, and any other monies that come due more than one year from the date of the statement.

MORTGAGE — Legal paper that pledges property to cover a debt.

NET WORTH — What the owner(s) has represented on a balance sheet as the difference between all assets and all liabilities, in other words, the owner's equity.

XYZ HARDWARE AND BUILDING SUPPLY
BALANCE SHEET
YEAR END 19XX

ASSETS		LIABILITIES	
CASH	$ 2,000	NOTES PAYABLE	$ 18,000
ACCTS REC	85,000	ACCTS PAYABLE	205,000
INVENTORY	210,000	ACCRUALS	6,000
TOTAL CURR ASSETS	297,000	TOTAL CURR LIABILITIES	229,000
LAND/BLDG	50,000	MORTGAGE	25,000
EQUIP/FIX	50,000		
TOTAL FIXED ASSETS	100,00	TOTAL LONG TERM DEBT	25,000
		NET WORTH	143,000
TOTAL ASSETS	397,000	TOTAL LIABILITIES &	
		NET WORTH	$397,000

Abbreviations used on the balance sheet are : ACCTS REC = accounts receivable; TOTAL CURR ASSETS = total current assets; LAND/BLDG = Land and Buildings; EQUIP/FIX = equipment and fixtures; ACCTS PAYABLE = accounts payable; TOTAL CURR LIABILITIES = total current liabilities.

GLOSSARY OF BASIC PROFIT AND LOSS STATEMENT TERMS

The Profit and Loss Statement that will be used as an example for the remainder of this book is shown on the facing page. Following are definitions of terms used in a Profit and Loss Statement.

NET SALES — The total dollar volume of all cash or credit sales less returns, allowances, discounts and rebates.

COST OF GOODS SOLD — For a retail or wholesale business it is the total price paid for the products sold plus the cost of having it delivered to the store during the accounting period.

For a manufacturing firm it is the beginning inventory plus purchases, delivery costs, material, labor, and overhead minus the ending inventory.

GROSS PROFIT — Profit before expenses and federal taxes have been deducted.

EXPENSES — The cost of doing business. It includes such items as: wages, telephone, insurance, depreciation, interest, and advertising.

NET PROFIT — The amount left over after expenses plus interest and federal taxes. (The term *net profit* as used in this book will always be profit before paying federal taxes).

THE P & L

PROFIT AND LOSS STATEMENT

NET SALES (LESS ALLOWANCES & DISCOUNTS)		$700,000
COST OF GOODS SOLD		500,000
GROSS PROFIT		200,000

EXPENSES

DRAWINGS (OWNERS)	$ 74,000
WAGES	65,000
DELIVERY	7,000
BAD DEBT	4,000
TELEPHONE	2,000
DEPRECIATION	4,000
INSURANCE	7,000
TAXES (LOCAL)	8,000
INTEREST	8,700
ADVERTISING	3,000
MISCELLANEOUS	2,000
TOTAL EXPENSES	$ 184,700

NET PROFIT (BEFORE FEDERAL TAXES)	$ 15,300

A LOOK AHEAD

To assess your basic financial understanding, five questions are listed below. These were designed to demonstrate that although the balance sheet and profit and loss statement contain considerable information, these instruments are only the launching pad of financial analysis. As we will soon learn, basic financial information can be used to develop simple ratios that will help you understand and control a business. Looking at your expenses as percents of sales can help you reduce your costs. And by keeping track of selected ratios and percentages over a period of time will help you chart the future with confidence.

Try the following questions. Don't worry if you can't answer them or don't understand them at this stage. By the end of this book you will!

FROM THE BALANCE SHEET AND PROFIT AND LOSS STATEMENT ON PAGES 13 AND 15 CAN YOU:

1. Observe that the owner can't pay current bills? (Hint - check the cash available.)

2. Calculate that the average collection period for A/R (accounts receivable) is over 30 days? (This will be covered in detail in Part III, efficiency ratios.)

3. Tell that the owner's return on investment (ROI) is less than what most experts say is necessary for future growth? (This will be apparent when you get to profitability ratios in Part III.)

4. Determine where the net profit is, since there is only $2,000 in cash? (Hint: it may be uncollected.)

5. See that the net worth of the owner is mainly composed of fixed assets? (This is what would be left when all debts are paid.)

The balance sheet and profit and loss statement alone do not provide sufficient financial information to properly operate a business. For instance, these documents cannot tell how long receivables have remained uncollected, what adding a new employee would do to cash flow, or how much money it takes to support a marketing plan.

The answer to these and other key questions comes from knowing how to use the information in a balance sheet and profit and loss statement. This is what you are about to learn in the pages ahead.

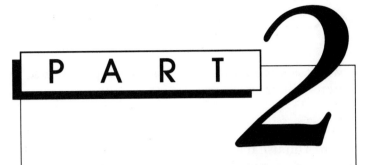

USING THE TOOLS OF THE TRADE

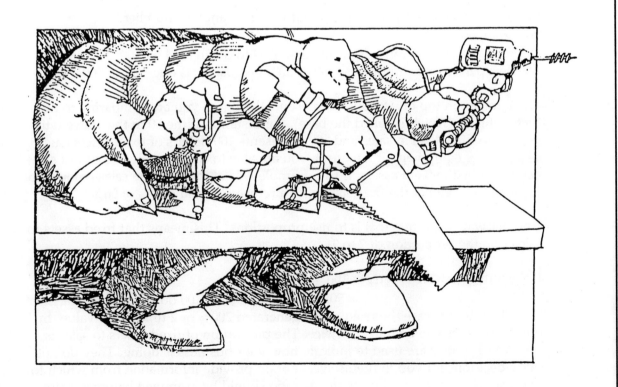

UNDERSTANDING RATIOS AND PERCENTAGES

Stay with this part. It is important. It may sound complex at first, but will become more clear as you use ratios.

Why Ratio Analysis?

Ratios are common. You use them everyday. They provide a better understanding of a wide range of situations. For instance, the miles you get per gallon (MPG) of gasoline or the unemployment rate presented as a ratio are easier to grasp than the total number of unemployed people or the total number of gallons of gas used. Ratios are used when we look for the best price per ounce for food, or when we compare batting averages of baseball players, or we measure the cost of a building by dollars per square foot.

Ratios are an even more important tool to measure the progress of a business and to compare a business to its competitors.

How Ratios Are Developed

Ratios are expressed by placing one number over another number.
For example: 50

  100 is a ratio. It means that 50 is to be divided by 100. The answer will be a percentage. In this case .50 or 50% because 50 is one-half of 100.

The number on top of a formula represents the figure you are comparing to the bottom figure (which is called the base). For instance, if the 50 in the above ratio represents 50 dollars in sales and 100 represents 100 dollars of fixed assets (such as a piece of equipment or a fixture), you are able to compare the amount of sales generated by the fixed assets. If this example was of interest, the sales amount to one-half the value of the fixed assets, or a return on fixed assets of 50%.

Another way to express this is to use proportions. This means that fixed assets to sales is in the proportion of 2 to 1.

If the numbers were reversed: 100

  50, then sales become 100 dollars and fixed assets 50 dollars. In this case the fixed assets generated 200% or 2 times their value. In other words, 50 can go into 100 twice. The proportion of fixed assets to sales is now 1 to 2. Ratios are used to indicate how your business is doing. They do not make decisions for you in themselves, but do provide information from which to make sound decisions. More than one ratio should be examined before a major decision is made, but more on this later. Right now, let's dig deeper into percentages and ratios.

What Ratios Measure

Ratios measure *proportions*. In our example of $\frac{100}{50}$ above, we were able to determine what proportion one figure is of another. Ratios also measure *relationships*. They do this because they can translate assets; such as tools and inventory, and liabilities; such as payables and loans, into common dollar figures. By doing this it is easy to see valuable relationships between two seemingly unrelated items. Ratios also allow you to make comparisions between time periods. For example, a ratio let's you measure your inventory turnover from one month to another, or year to year.

The 10% Paradox

Suppose you are asked if you would be willing to take a chance on an event that would pay you $100,000. All you had to do was call "heads or tails" at the fair flip of a coin. Probability laws tell you that you have a 50–50 chance of winning. But, suppose you have to risk $10,000 (10%) to participate in the coin flip? You might shy away putting $10,000 at risk even though the pay off was large. However, you might be willing to risk less to get less, i.e. 10% of $1,000 or $100. In other words, even though the percentage did not change, spending a large amount of "real" money would make the difference. Ratios and percentages, therefore, need to be kept in context as to what they represent.

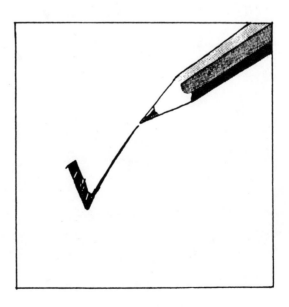

USING RATIOS WITHOUT FEAR

Think of a ratio as a friend when scrutinizing your business. Ratios are simple to calculate, especially with a hand held calculator, and easy to use. They provide a wealth of information that cannot be gotten anywhere else.

Ratios cannot take the place of experience or replace good management, but they will make good managers better. Ratios can help to point out areas that need more investigating or assist in developing future operating strategy.

You can quickly learn to use a number of ratios by following the steps outlined in this book. The "fill-in-the-blank" forms presented later, will assist you in analyzing any business. Going through the forms provided should allow you to understand basic ratios and be comfortable using them.

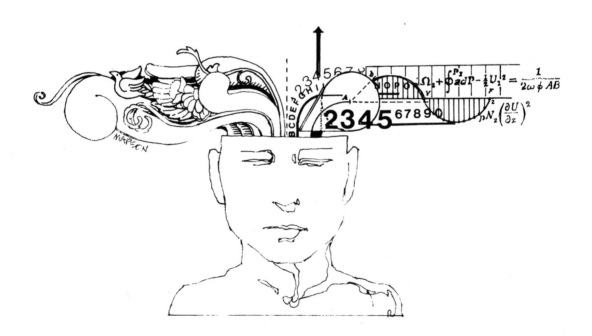

BASIC RULES FOR RATIOS

To ease you into the use of ratios, carefully review the following five basic rules:

1. To determine a percentage change suppose your sales increased 25% the first month of the year and 37% the second month. It would be wrong to state the second month's increase was 12%. This is because both were taken from the same base period (in this case 100). Therefore this is a 12 percentage **points** increase. To determine the actual monthly increase, the 12 point increase of the second month should be divided by the new base period of 125 (the beginning figure plus the first month's increase) for a true monthly increase of 9.5%

2. When comparing a part to a whole such as net profits to sales, the whole is always the base. That is
$$\frac{\text{net profits}}{\text{sales}}$$

3. A percent of something can **increase** by more than 100% but cannot **decrease** by more than 100%. Think of it like this: you can double your money, (200%), but can lose 100% of it only once.

4. Ratios lose significance and accuracy when they become excessively detailed. This is important because it means that you don't need a lot of detailed data or figures to use ratio analysis. Analysis is often significant when used in general ways (i.e. ''ballpark'' figures.)

5. Remember that ratios will assist you in decision making not make the decisions for you.

Cautions To Keep In Mind When Using Ratios

Maintain An Objective Attitude. Don't use ratios to support predetermined conclusions. Use them to help you better understand your business.

Don't Use The Wrong Figures. For instance when looking at a percent change between two dollar figures, such as a raise in price from $2.00 to $3.00, the number you want to compare is the **difference** between the two dollar figures which is $1.00. This difference figure ($1.00) is then divided by $2.00 for a percent raise of 50%. Don't divide $2.00 by $3.00 or vice versa.

Don't Compare Meaningless Numbers. For example, compare expenses to fixed assets. This number is easy to calculate but has no meaning in the operation of a business.

SUMMARY OF THE TOOLS OF THE TRADE

- You have been introduced to ratio analysis and now know that ratios are expressed as a percent or a proportion.

- You discovered that ratios are developed by dividing the number you wish to compare by the base number.

- You have regularly used ratios in many home and business transactions. These are developed the same way as ratios we will learn to use in the book.

- You learned that ratios are expressed like this:*

$$\frac{50}{100} = 50\% \text{ or 1 to 2 (1:2) and}$$

$$\frac{100}{50} = 2 \text{ Times or 2 to 1 (2:1)}$$

- You discovered that ratios can be easy to develop and use and noted a few basic rules and cautions that will enable you to understand them better.

- Finally, we hope you know that ratios are a friend and can help you control your business.

---

*HINT: If the top number is smaller than the bottom number, the ratio will be a percent. If the top number is larger than the bottom number the ratio will be expressed as ''Times''.

PART 3

THREE TYPES OF RATIOS
- **LIQUIDITY**
- **PROFITABILITY**
- **EFFICIENCY**

INTRODUCTION TO RATIOS

This part of the book presents and explains several common ratios that can be used to measure and control a business. You will not use every ratio that is presented, especially if you are in a service business. It is not necessary to memorize the ratios or their meanings presented in this part, because you can always return to this part of the book for reference.

The first set of ratios are called *liquidity ratios* because they measure the amount of cash available to cover expenses, both current and long term. These ratios are especially important in keeping a business alive. Not paying your bills due to a shortage of cash is the fastest way to go out of business. Lending institutions often don't want to loan money when it is actually needed. Make arrangements ahead of time for a line-of-credit. The best time to do this is when your business liquidity looks very good. Make sure your line of credit agreement is always in writing!

The second set of ratios is called *profitability ratios.* These ratios measure and help control income. This is done through higher sales, larger margins, getting more from your expenses, and/or a combination of these methods.

The third set of ratios is called *efficiency ratios.* Efficiency ratios measure and help control the operation of the business. They add another dimension to help you increase income by assessing such important transactions as the use of credit, control of inventory, and/or management of assets.

GLOSSARY FOR RATIO ANALYSIS

CURRENT ASSETS — The sum of cash, notes, and accounts receivable (less reserves for bad debts), advances on inventories, inventories, and any other thing that can be converted into cash in a short time, usually less than a year.

CURRENT LIABILITIES — The total of all monies owed by the company that will fall due within one year.

SALES — (or net sales) The total dollar volume of all sales less returns, allowances, discounts, and rebates.

WORKING CAPITAL — Current assets less current liabilities.

TOTAL DEBT — The sum of all liabilities both current and long term.

NET WORTH — What the owner(s) have represented on a balance sheeet as the difference between all assets and all liabilities.

EARNINGS BEFORE INTEREST AND TAXES (EBIT) — Net profit before all interest payments and federal taxes.

NET PROFIT — The amount left over after expenses plus interest and federal taxes. (The term net profit as used in this book will always be before federal taxes).

TOTAL ASSETS — The sum of all current and fixed assets.

ACCOUNTS RECEIVABLE — Credit sales dollars not yet collected.

COST OF GOODS SOLD — For a retail or wholesale business, it is the total price paid for the products sold plus the cost of having it delivered to the store, during the accounting period.

For a manufacturing firm, it is the beginning inventory plus purchases, delivery costs, material, labor, and overhead minus the ending inventory.

(continued next page)

GLOSSARY (Continued)

INVENTORY — For a manufacturing firm it is the sum of finished merchandise on hand, raw material, and material in process.

For retailers and wholesalers, it is the stock of salable goods on hand.

FIXED ASSETS — Land, buildings, building equipment, fixtures, machinery, tools, furniture, office devices, patterns, and drawings, less salvage value and depreciation.

Ratio #1: Liquidity Ratios

The next several pages will present three useful liquidity ratios. They will be shown with a balance sheet and profit and loss statement on the left page and an explanation of what the ratios mean and how to use them on the facing right page.

To fit all the information on the page, some abbreviations are used.

These abbreviations are explained below:

ACCTS REC = accounts receivable

TOTAL CURR ASSETS = total current assets

LAND/BLDG = land and buildings

EQUIP/FIX = equipment and fixtures

TOTAL CA AND FA = total current assets and fixed assets

ACCTS PAYABLE = accounts payable

TOTAL CURR LIABILITIES = total current liabilities

TOTAL LIAB AND NW = total liabilities and net worth.

NOTE: Each figure used to develop a ratio will be highlighted on the Balance Sheet or P & L Statement to show exactly where it came from by using a shaded area.

XYZ HARDWARE AND BUILDING SUPPLY
BALANCE SHEET
YEAR END 19XX

ASSETS			LIABILITIES		
CASH	$ 2,000		NOTES PAYABLE	$ 18,000	
ACCTS REC	85,000		ACCTS PAYABLE	205,000	
INVENTORY	210,000		ACCRUALS	6,000	
TOTAL CURR ASSETS		297,000	TOTAL CURR LIABILITIES		229,000
LAND/BLDG	50,000		MORTGAGE	25,000	
EQUIP/FIX	50,000				
TOTAL FIXED ASSETS		100,000	TOTAL LONG TERM DEBT		25,000
			NET WORTH		143,000
TOTAL CA AND FA		$397,000	TOTAL LIAB AND NW		$397,000

PROFIT AND LOSS STATEMENT

NET SALES (LESS ALLOW & DISCOUNTS)	$700,000
COST OF GOODS SOLD	500,000
GROSS PROFIT	200,000

EXPENSES

DRAWINGS (OWNER)	$ 74,000
WAGES	65,000
DELIVERY	7,000
BAD DEBT	4,000
TELEPHONE	2,000
DEPRECIATION	4,000
INSURANCE	7,000
TAXES (LOCAL)	8,000
INTEREST	8,700
ADVERTISING	3,000
MISCELLANEOUS	2,000
TOTAL EXPENSES	$184,700

NET PROFIT (BEFORE FEDERAL TAXES)	$ 15,300

RATIO: CURRENT RATIO

$$\frac{\text{CURRRENT ASSETS} \quad \$297,000}{\text{CURRENT LIABILITIES} \quad \$229,000} = 1.3 \text{ Times}$$

CURRENT RATIO

MEASURES: The ability to meet short term obligations.

GENERALLY ACCEPTED STANDARD: Current assets should be 2 times or 200% of current liabilities.

LOW RATIO: A company may not be able to pay off bills as rapidly as it should. It may not be able to take advantage of cash discounts or other favorable terms. It may not be able to keep its suppliers happy and receive eager service. High inventory means high accounts payable.

HIGH RATIO: Money that could be working for the business is tied up in government securities, cash savings, or other safe funds.

REMARKS: The proper ratio depends on the type of business, the time in the business cycle, and the age of the business. You need to inquire about what is proper in your type of business.

QUICK RATIO: Another variation is the quick ratio (or acid test) which is the same as the current ratio except it eliminates inventory so that only cash and accounts receivable assets are counted. Some analysts reduce accounts receivable by 25% before using this ratio. Whether you do or not depends on how much faith you have in your ability to collect your debts. The ratio looks like this:

$$\frac{cash + accounts\ receivable}{current\ liabilities} \quad or \quad \frac{87,000^*}{229,000} = 38\%$$

A safe margin would be at least 1.0 times. The example shown above is less than one-half to one, and suggests some serious problems such as slow moving inventory.

```
* Cash —      $ 2,000
  Accts Rec — $85,000
              $87,000
```

XYZ HARDWARE AND BUILDING SUPPLY
BALANCE SHEET
YEAR END 19XX

ASSETS			LIABILITIES		
CASH	$ 2,000		NOTES PAYABLE	$ 18,000	
ACCTS REC	85,000		ACCTS PAYABLE	205,000	
INVENTORY	210,000		ACCRUALS	6,000	
TOTAL CURR ASSETS		297,000	TOTAL CURR LIABILITIES		229,000
LAND/BLDG	50,000		MORTGAGE	25,000	
EQUIP/FIX	50,000				
TOTAL FIXED ASSETS		100,000	TOTAL LONG TERM DEBT		25,000
			NET WORTH		143,000
TOTAL CA AND FA		$397,000	TOTAL LIAB AND NW		$397,000

PROFIT AND LOSS STATEMENT

NET SALES (LESS ALLOW & DISCOUNTS)		$700,000
COST OF GOODS SOLD		500,000
GROSS PROFIT		200,000

EXPENSES

DRAWINGS (OWNER)	$ 74,000	
WAGES	65,000	
DELIVERY	7,000	
BAD DEBT	4,000	
TELEPHONE	2,000	
DEPRECIATION	4,000	
INSURANCE	7,000	
TAXES (LOCAL)	8,000	
INTEREST	8,700	
ADVERTISING	3,000	
MISCELLANEOUS	2,000	
TOTAL EXPENSES	$184,700	
NET PROFIT (BEFORE FEDERAL TAXES)		$ 15,300

RATIO: TURNOVER OF CASH

$$\frac{\text{SALES}}{\text{WORKING CAPITAL}} \quad \frac{700,000}{68,000*} = 10.3 \text{ Times}$$

*(Working capital = current assets − current liabilities) $297,000 − $229,000 = $68,000

TURNOVER OF CASH RATIO

NOTE: It's called working capital because it is the amount necessary to operate your business on a daily basis. Working capital is the money you use for salaries, to pay your bills, etc. The amount of your working capital changes every time you receive cash, make a cash sale, or write a check.

MEASURES: The turnover of cash or working capital. Maintaining a positive cash flow or working capital balance will provide an adequate means to finance your sales without struggling to pay for the material and or goods you are buying.

GENERALLY ACCEPTED STANDARD: Sales should be 5 or 6 times of working capital.

LOW RATIO: You may have funds tied up in short-term low-yielding assets. This means that you may get by on less cash.

HIGH RATIO: A vulnerability to creditors, such as the inability to pay wages or utility bills.

REMARKS: Usually, if the current assets/current liabilities ratio is low, the turnover of cash ratio will be high. This is due to the small amount of working capital that is available.

XYZ HARDWARE AND BUILDING SUPPLY
BALANCE SHEET
YEAR END 19XX

ASSETS			LIABILITIES		
CASH	$ 2,000		NOTES PAYABLE	$ 18,000	
ACCTS REC	85,000		ACCTS PAYABLE	205,000	
INVENTORY	210,000		ACCRUALS	6,000	
TOTAL CURR ASSETS		297,000	TOTAL CURR LIABILITIES		229,000
LAND/BLDG	50,000		MORTGAGE	25,000	PLUS
EQUIP/FIX	50,000				
TOTAL FIXED ASSETS		100,000	TOTAL LONG TERM DEBT		25,000
			NET WORTH		143,000
TOTAL CA AND FA		$397,000	TOTAL LIAB AND NW		$397,000

PROFIT AND LOSS STATEMENT

NET SALES (LESS ALLOW & DISCOUNTS)		$700,000
COST OF GOODS SOLD		500,000
GROSS PROFIT		200,000

EXPENSES

DRAWINGS (OWNER)	$ 74,000	
WAGES	65,000	
DELIVERY	10,000	
BAD DEBT	4,000	
TELEPHONE	2,000	
DEPRECIATION	4,000	
INSURANCE	7,000	
TAXES (LOCAL)	8,000	
INTEREST	2,700	
ADVERTISING	3,000	
MISCELLANEOUS	2,000	
TOTAL EXPENSES	$184,700	

NET PROFIT (BEFORE FEDERAL TAXES) $ 15,300

RATIO: DEBT TO NET WORTH

$$\frac{\text{TOTAL DEBT}}{\text{NET WORTH}} \quad \frac{254,000 \ (229,000 + 25,000)}{143,000} = 1.8 \text{ Times}$$

DEBT TO NET WORTH RATIO

MEASURES: Total debt coverage expresses the relationship between capital contributed by the creditors and that contributed by the owner(s).

GENERALLY ACCEPTED STANDARD: Current liabilities should not be less than 1.25 times net worth or the creditors may want as much to say about the operation of your business as you. Some analysts feel that **current liabilities** to net worth shouldn't exceed 80% and **long term debt** should not exceed net worth by 50%.

LOW RATIO: Greater long term financial safety. This would generally mean you have greater flexibility to borrow money. An extremely low ratio may mean that the firm's management is too conservative. This may indicate the firm is not reaching its full profit potential, that is, the profit potential from **leverage**, which is realized by borrowing money at a low rate of interest and obtaining a higher rate of return on sales.

HIGH RATIO: Greater risk being assumed by the creditors, hence greater interest by them in the way the firm is being manager. Your ability to obtain money from outside sources is limited.

REMARKS: Again, a lot depends on where business is in its life cycle, what the policies of the owners are, the state of the economy, and the particular business cycle. Remember long term debt is leverage. Leverage can work for you during the good time and against you during a sales slump. This can create decreased earnings if too much money is borrowed.

SUMMARY OF LIQUIDITY RATIOS

Having read this far you are well on your way to mastering the use of ratios analysis.

- Liquidity ratios help you determine your firm's ability to pay debts.

- The current ratio is important as it provides an indication of your ability to pay your immediate bills.

- Working capital is the difference between current assets and current liabilities. This is an important figure because it represents the amount available to pay for salaries or new material or goods.

- By maintaining a proper ratio for your turnover of cash you will be able to take advantage of discounts for prompt payment.

- Your total debt should not exceed 80% of your net worth and your long term debt should not exceed 50% of your net worth.

Ratio #2: Profitability Ratios

Profitability is why most of us are in business. We want a better return for our money and time than we can get from a bank or other low-risk interest-paying opportunity. This, by the way, is one of the most commonly used methods to evaluate whether you are doing well with your business. For example, if savings accounts or money market accounts are paying a higher percent than you are earning on the money you have invested in your business, you will probably want to consider selling your business and reinvesting your money elsewhere unless you particularly like your line of work better than making more money. Profitability ratios provide you with the means to measure your earnings in several ways (as we will soon see). They measure your profit margin, return on assets, return on investment, and return on sales.

As a general rule, profitability, or income, as it is sometimes called, comes about from changes in price or volume or both. Therefore, changes of your ratios over time will come about by what you do that affects changes in your price and/or volume. This will be noted by increases in expenses such as for more salespeople or advertising, changes will take place as assets are depreciated, or new ones are added, or if borrowing takes place. If you raise or lower your prices, changes will usually be shown by changes in your ratios.

Abbreviations used on the balance sheet are: ACCTS REC = accounts receivable;   TOTAL CURR ASSETS = total current assets;   LAND/BLDG = land and buildings;   EQUIP/FIX = equipment and fixtures;   TOTAL CA AND FA = total current assets and fixed assets;   ACCTS PAYABLE = accounts payable;   TOTAL CURR LIABILITIES = total current liabilities;   TOTAL LIAB AND NW = total liabilities and net worth.

NOTE: Each figure used to develop a ratio will be highlighted on the Balance Sheet or P & L Statement to show exactly where it came from by using a shaded area.

XYZ HARDWARE AND BUILDING SUPPLY
BALANCE SHEET
YEAR END 19XX

ASSETS			LIABILITIES		
CASH	$ 2,000		NOTES PAYABLE	$ 18,000	
ACCTS REC	85,000		ACCTS PAYABLE	205,000	
INVENTORY	210,000		ACCRUALS	6,000	
TOTAL CURR ASSETS		297,000	TOTAL CURR LIABILITIES		229,000
LAND/BLDG	50,000		MORTGAGE	25,000	
EQUIP/FIX	50,000				
TOTAL FIXED ASSETS		100,000	TOTAL LONG TERM DEBT		25,000
			NET WORTH		143,000
TOTAL CA AND FA		$397,000	TOTAL LIAB AND NW		$397,000

PROFIT AND LOSS STATEMENT

NET SALES (LESS ALLOW & DISCOUNTS)	$700,000
COST OF GOODS SOLD	500,000
GROSS PROFIT	200,000

EXPENSES

DRAWINGS (OWNER)	$ 74,000
WAGES	65,000
DELIVERY	7,000
BAD DEBT	4,000
TELEPHONE	2,000
DEPRECIATION	4,000
INSURANCE	7,000
TAXES (LOCAL)	8,000
INTEREST	8,700
ADVERTISING	3,000
MISCELLANEOUS	2,000
TOTAL EXPENSES	184,700

PLUS

NET PROFIT (BEFORE FEDERAL TAXES)	$ 15,300

RATIO: NET PROFIT

$$\frac{\text{EARNINGS BEFORE INTEREST AND TAXES (EBIT)*}}{\text{NET SALES}} = \frac{24,000 \ (15,300 + 8,700)}{700,000} = 3.4\%$$

*Taxes as used here mean federal taxes.

NET PROFIT RATIO

MEASURES: The effectiveness of management. This is a valid comparison between firms in the same industry. This ratio filters any distortions that may occur because of high debt or other factors that may affect the tax payments or lack of tax payments.

GENERALLY ACCEPTED STANDARDS: Depends on the business and/or industry. The volume of business is also an important factor as well as the age of your business.

LOW RATIO: Perhaps the expenses of doing business are too great; there are inefficiencies; or sales are too low for the costs.

HIGH RATIO: There is a high earnings margin or expenses are being held down.

REMARKS: The measure of what is a good ratio is dependent on the type of business or industry. This should be compared to the industry standards. Earnings before interest and taxes (EBIT) are also called operating income.

This ratio does not consider any investment made in buildings, machinery, etc. The investment turnover ratio on page 52, considers these types of capital investments, but it does not consider expenses.

XYZ HARDWARE AND BUILDING SUPPLY
BALANCE SHEET
YEAR END 19XX

ASSETS			LIABILITIES		
CASH	$ 2,000		NOTES PAYABLE	$ 18,000	
ACCTS REC	85,000		ACCTS PAYABLE	205,000	
INVENTORY	210,000		ACCRUALS	6,000	
TOTAL CURR ASSETS		297,000	TOTAL CURR LIABILITIES		229,000
LAND/BLDG	50,000		MORTGAGE	25,000	
EQUIP/FIX	50,000				
TOTAL FIXED ASSETS		100,000	TOTAL LONG TERM DEBT		25,000
			NET WORTH		143,000
TOTAL CA AND FA		$397,000	TOTAL LIAB AND NW		$397,000

PROFIT AND LOSS STATEMENT

NET SALES (LESS ALLOW & DISCOUNTS)	$700,000
COST OF GOODS SOLD	500,000
GROSS PROFIT	200,000

EXPENSES

DRAWINGS (OWNER)	$ 74,000
WAGES	65,000
DELIVERY	7,000
BAD DEBT	4,000
TELEPHONE	2,000
DEPRECIATION	4,000
INSURANCE	7,000
TAXES (LOCAL)	8,000
INTEREST	8,700
ADVERTISING	3,000
MISCELLANEOUS	5,000
TOTAL EXPENSES	$184,700
NET PROFIT (BEFORE FEDERAL TAXES)	$ 15,300

RATIO: RATE OF RETURN ON SALES

$$\frac{\text{NET PROFIT}}{\text{NET SALES}} \quad \frac{15,300}{700,000} \quad = \quad 2.2\%$$

RATE OF RETURN ON SALES RATIO

MEASURES: How much net profit was derived from every dollar of sales. It indicates how well you have managed your operating expenses. It may also indicate whether the business is generating enough sales to cover the fixed costs and still leave an acceptable profit.

GENERALLY ACCEPTED STANDARD: Depends on the business and/or the industry. Price and volume are important and play a large role in determining this ratio.

LOW RATIO: May not mean too much in some industries; for instance business that has a high turnover of inventory or one that uses low margin to attract business such as a grocery store might show a low ratio, but still be healthy.

HIGH RATIO: Usually the higher the ratio the better. However, if you are beating last year's figures and show a steady increase, you are on the right track.

REMARKS: In analyzing your business, this ratio must be viewed with many facts in mind and used in conjunction with other ratios and analytical tools. Beware of using this ratio alone, as you can easily begin comparing apples and oranges. Comparing it with your own results month after month or year after year, is valid.

XYZ HARDWARE AND BUILDING SUPPLY
BALANCE SHEET
YEAR END 19XX

ASSETS			LIABILITIES		
CASH	$ 2,000		NOTES PAYABLE	$ 18,000	
ACCTS REC	85,000		ACCTS PAYABLE	205,000	
INVENTORY	210,000		ACCRUALS	6,000	
TOTAL CURR ASSETS		297,000	TOTAL CURR LIABILITIES		229,000
LAND/BLDG	50,000		MORTGAGE	25,000	
EQUIP/FIX	50,000				
TOTAL FIXED ASSETS		100,000	TOTAL LONG TERM DEBT		25,000
			NET WORTH		143,000
TOTAL CA AND FA		$397,000	TOTAL LIAB AND NW		$397,000

PROFIT AND LOSS STATEMENT

NET SALES (LESS ALLOW & DISCOUNTS)	$700,000
COST OF GOODS SOLD	500,000
GROSS PROFIT	200,000

EXPENSES

DRAWINGS (OWNER)	$ 74,000
WAGES	65,000
DELIVERY	7,000
BAD DEBT	4,000
TELEPHONE	2,000
DEPRECIATION	4,000
INSURANCE	7,000
TAXES (LOCAL)	8,000
INTEREST	8,700
ADVERTISING	3,000
MISCELLANEOUS	2,000
TOTAL EXPENSES	$184,700

NET PROFIT (BEFORE FEDERAL TAXES) $ 15,300

RATIO: RETURN ON INVESTMENT (ROI)

$$\frac{\text{NET PROFIT}}{\text{NET WORTH}} \quad \frac{15,300}{143,000} \quad = \quad 10.7\%$$

RETURN ON INVESTMENT RATIO (ROI)

MEASURES: Return on the owners investment (ROI). Some use this figure as a final evaluation.

GENERALLY ACCEPTED STANDARD: A relationship of at least 14% is generally considered necessary to fund future growth.

LOW RATIO: Perhaps you could have done better investing your money in savings bonds or some other investment opportunity. This could indicate inefficient management performance or it could reflect a highly capitalized, conservatively operated business.

HIGH RATIO: Perhaps creditors were a source of much of the funds, or management is efficient, or the firm is undercapitalized.

REMARKS: This measure is considered one of the best criteria of profitability; it can be a key ratio to compare against other firms or the industry average. However, it should be used in conjuction with other ratios. There should be a direct relationship between ROI and risk; that is, the greater the risk, the higher the return. Remember, net worth is the difference between assets and liabilities. A smaller net worth figure would equate to a higher ratio.

Another measure of ROI is: $\dfrac{\text{EBIT*}}{\text{NET WORTH}} = \dfrac{24{,}000}{143{,}000} = 16.7\%$

NOTE: The above is a combination of the profitability ratio called *net profit* (page 36) and the efficiency ratio called *investment turnover,* (page 52). This ratio overcomes the shortcomings of both. But don't fail to look at each separately to tell what might have caused any changes: increased income from more sales or better utilization of your assets.

*EBIT = earnings before interest and taxes

42

XYZ HARDWARE AND BUILDING SUPPLY
BALANCE SHEET
YEAR END 19XX

ASSETS			LIABILITIES		
CASH	$ 2,000		NOTES PAYABLE	$ 18,000	
ACCTS REC	85,000		ACCTS PAYABLE	205,000	
INVENTORY	210,000		ACCRUALS	6,000	
TOTAL CURR ASSETS		297,000	TOTAL CURR LIABILITIES		229,000
LAND/BLDG	50,000		MORTGAGE	25,000	
EQUIP/FIX	50,000				
TOTAL FIXED ASSETS		100,000	TOTAL LONG TERM DEBT		25,000
			NET WORTH		143,000
TOTAL CA AND FA		$397,000	TOTAL LIAB AND NW		$397,000

PROFIT AND LOSS STATEMENT

NET SALES (LESS ALLOW & DISCOUNTS)		$700,000
COST OF GOODS SOLD		500,000
GROSS PROFIT		200,000

EXPENSES

DRAWINGS (OWNER)	$ 74,000
WAGES	65,000
DELIVERY	7,000
BAD DEBT	4,000
TELEPHONE	2,000
DEPRECIATION	4,000
INSURANCE	7,000
TAXES (LOCAL)	8,000
INTEREST	8,700
ADVERTISING	3,000
MISCELLANEOUS	2,000
TOTAL EXPENSES	$184,700

NET PROFIT (BEFORE FEDERAL TAXES) $ 15,300

RATIO: RATE OF RETURN ON ASSETS

$$\frac{\text{NET PROFIT}}{\text{TOTAL ASSETS}} = \frac{15,300}{397,000} = 3.8\%$$

RATE OF RETURN ON ASSETS RATIO

MEASURES: The profit that is generated by the use of the assets of the business.

GENERALLY ACCEPTED STANDARD: Varies a great deal depending on the industry and the amount of fixed assets that must be used, the amount of cash that must be available, etc.

LOW RATIO: Poor performance, or ineffective employment of the assets by management.

HIGH RATIO: Good performance, or effective use of the firm's assets by management.

REMARKS: This ratio can easily be distorted by a heavily depreciated plant, a large amount of intangible assets, or unusual income or expense items. This ratio should be used with other ratios to compare firms in the same industry and of approximately the same size. It is a valid tool if you know the real value of your competitor's assets (especially fixed assets) and whether they are including outside earnings as a large part of their current assets. If you don't know, beware of making a firm conclusion from this ratio alone.

A variation of this ratio would be to split the assets into fixed and current and work a ratio on each of them. Knowing the return on fixed assets could be important to a business that has to count on a heavy investment in fixed assets such as rolling stock or heavy machinery to generate sales and profits.

SUMMARY OF PROFITABILITY RATIOS

- Profitability ratios measure profit margin, return on assets, return on investment, and return on sales.

- Profitability is a result of several things such as: your price structure, the amount of business you do, and how well you control your expenses.

- The net profit ratio is a valid ratio to compare your business to your industry average.

- Your return on investment can be compare as a return on net worth or total assets.

- The rate of return on sales must be used with caution when comparing your business with that of others.

- Beware of using the rate of return on total assets ratio to compare your business with others without knowing: The condition of the fixed assets; if the fixed assets are leased; and if outside earnings are a part of current assets.

Ratio #3: Efficiency Ratios

Efficiency ratios measure how well you are conducting your business. These ratios provide an indication of how fast you are collecting your money for credit sales and how many times you are turning over your inventory in a given period of time. They measure the amount of sales generated by your assets and the return you are earning on your assets.

Efficiency ratios are an important landmark to keeping your business in balance. For instance, if you become too loose in offering credit to generate sales, this will show up as an increase in the average number of days it takes to collect your accounts receivable. If you over-buy, even with well-meaning intentions of not passing up a real bargain, this will be reflected in a decrease in the turnover of your inventory. Similarly, if you acquire too many fixed assets without a corresponding increase in sales this ratio will quickly remind you of less sales generated by your assets.

Of course other ratios will also play a part in maintaining a balance in your business that will aid you in maintaining healthy growth, but the efficiency ratios will usually note it sooner. You will notice that some efficiency ratios are in days and not percentages or proportions.

Abbreviations used on the balance sheet are: ACCTS REC = accounts receivable;   TOTAL CURR ASSETS = total current assets; LAND/BLDG = land and buildings;   EQUIP/FIX = equipment and fixtures;   TOTAL CA AND FA = total current assets and fixed assets; ACCTS PAYABLE = accounts payable;   TOTAL CURR LIABILITIES = total current liabilities;   TOTAL LIAB AND NW = total liabilities and net worth.

XYZ HARDWARE AND BUILDING SUPPLY
BALANCE SHEET
YEAR END 19XX

ASSETS			LIABILITIES		
CASH	$ 2,000		NOTES PAYABLE	$ 18,000	
ACCTS REC	85,000		ACCTS PAYABLE	205,000	
INVENTORY	210,000		ACCRUALS	6,000	
TOTAL CURR ASSETS		297,000	TOTAL CURR LIABILITIES		229,000
LAND/BLDG	50,000		MORTGAGE	25,000	
EQUIP/FIX	50,000				
TOTAL FIXED ASSETS		100,000	TOTAL LONG TERM DEBT		25,000
			NET WORTH		143,000
TOTAL CA AND FA		$397,000	TOTAL LIAB AND NW		$397,000

PROFIT AND LOSS STATEMENT

NET SALES (LESS ALLOW & DISCOUNTS)	$700,000	
COST OF GOODS SOLD	500,000	
GROSS PROFIT	200,000	

EXPENSES

DRAWINGS (OWNER)	$ 74,000
WAGES	65,000
DELIVERY	7,000
BAD DEBT	4,000
TELEPHONE	2,000
DEPRECIATION	4,000
INSURANCE	7,000
TAXES (LOCAL)	8,000
INTEREST	8,700
ADVERTISING	3,000
MISCELLANEOUS	2,000
TOTAL EXPENSES	$184,700

NET PROFIT (BEFORE FEDERAL TAXES) $ 15,300

RATIO: AVERAGE COLLECTION PERIOD FOR ACCOUNTS RECEIVABLE

$$\frac{\text{ACCOUNTS RECEIVABLE} \times 365 \text{ DAYS/YEAR}}{\text{SALES}} \qquad \frac{85,000 \times 365}{700,000*} \quad = \quad 44 \text{ DAYS}$$

*NOTE: Purposes here assume that all sales were credit sales.

AVERAGE COLLECTION PERIOD RATIO

MEASURES: The turnover of receivables – the average period of time it takes to collect your credit sales dollars.

GENERALLY ACCEPTED STANDARD: Depends on your collection period policy . . . if it is thirty days, then thirty days is the standard.

HIGH RATIO: A slow turnover – which may be the result of a number of bad accounts, or a tax collection policy, or perhaps credit is being used to generate sales.

LOW RATIO: A fast turnover – which could be the result of a stringent collection policy or fast-paying customers.

REMARKS: Generally anything within 10-15 days of *your* collection period is deemed acceptable and considered within the collection period.

NOTE: Another variation is shown below. It's a two step process that first measures your average daily credit sales and then provides the average collection period. If average daily credit sales are important, then use this ratio—if not, the other is easier and quicker to use. Both provide the same answer.

$$\frac{\text{Net Credit Sales}}{365} = \frac{700,000}{365} = \$1,918 = \textbf{Daily Credit Sales}$$

$$\frac{\text{Accounts Receivable}}{\textbf{Daily Credit Sales}} = \frac{85,000}{1,918} = 44 \text{ Days} = \text{Average Collection Period}$$

XYZ HARDWARE AND BUILDING SUPPLY
BALANCE SHEET
YEAR END 19XX

ASSETS			LIABILITIES		
CASH	$ 2,000		NOTES PAYABLE	$ 18,000	
ACCTS REC	85,000		ACCTS PAYABLE	205,000	
INVENTORY	210,000		ACCRUALS	6,000	
TOTAL CURR ASSETS		297,000	TOTAL CURR LIABILITIES		229,000
LAND/BLDG	50,000		MORTGAGE	25,000	
EQUIP/FIX	50,000				
TOTAL FIXED ASSETS		100,000	TOTAL LONG TERM DEBT		25,000
			NET WORTH		143,000
TOTAL CA AND FA		$397,000	TOTAL LIAB AND NW		$397,000

PROFIT AND LOSS STATEMENT

NET SALES (LESS ALLOW & DISCOUNTS)	$700,000
COST OF GOODS SOLD	500,000
GROSS PROFIT	200,000

EXPENSES

DRAWINGS (OWNER)	$ 74,000
WAGES	65,000
DELIVERY	7,000
BAD DEBT	4,000
TELEPHONE	2,000
DEPRECIATION	4,000
INSURANCE	7,000
TAXES (LOCAL)	8,000
INTEREST	8,700
ADVERTISING	3,000
MISCELLANEOUS	2,000
TOTAL EXPENSES	$184,700

NET PROFIT (BEFORE FEDERAL TAXES) $ 15,300

RATIO: INVENTORY TURNOVER _____ **ALSO CALLED THE STOCK TO SALES RATIO**

$$\frac{\text{COST-OF-GOODS-SOLD}}{\text{AVERAGE INVENTORY}} \quad \frac{500,000}{210,000} = 2.4 \text{ TIMES} \quad (152 \text{ DOH})^*$$

OR

$$\frac{\text{NET SALES}}{\text{AVERAGE INVENTORY}} \quad \frac{700,000}{210,000} = 3.3 \text{ TIMES} \quad (110 \text{ DOH})^*$$

*DOH = days on hand, see remarks next page
The cost-of-goods-sold figure is used by some analysts because most inventories are carried on the balance sheet by how much they cost, not the selling price, which is shown by using net sales.

INVENTORY TURNOVER RATIO

> **NOTE:** Manufacturers inventory = finished goods, raw material, and in-process material.
>
> Retailers/wholesalers inventory = saleable goods on hand.

MEASURES: Inventory turnover. This shows how fast your merchandise is moving. That is, how many times your initial inventory is replaced in a month/year.

GENERALLY ACCEPTED STANDARD: Depends on the industry and even the time of year for some industries. However 6 to 7 times is a rule of thumb.

LOW RATIO: An indication of a large inventory, a never-out-of-stock situation, perhaps some obsolete items, or it could indicate poor liquidity, some possible overstocking of items, or a planned buildup in anticipation of a coming high-selling period.

HIGH RATIO: An indication of a narrow selection, maybe fast-moving merchandise, or perhaps some lost sales. It may indicate better liquidity, maybe superior merchandising, or a shortage of inventory needed for sales.

REMARKS: Faster turnovers are generally viewed as a positive trend; they increase cash flow, reduce warehousing, etc. This ratio measures how management is using inventory and can be used to compare one period to the next or to another company in the same industry or the industry average. Again, it's an indicator, not an absolute measure or count. As a general rule a small retail business should not carry more than 100% of its working capital in inventory.

> **NOTE:**
>
> **(DOH):** Another measure is to make the inventory turnover (I T) ratio and divide it into 365 days:
>
> $$\frac{365}{I\ T} = \text{the average number of days the inventory is on hand.}$$
>
> $$\frac{365}{2.4} = 152 \text{ days on hand.}$$

XYZ HARDWARE AND BUILDING SUPPLY
BALANCE SHEET
YEAR END 19XX

ASSETS			LIABILITIES		
CASH	$ 2,000		NOTES PAYABLE	$ 18,000	
ACCTS REC	85,000		ACCTS PAYABLE	205,000	
INVENTORY	210,000		ACCRUALS	6,000	
TOTAL CURR ASSETS		297,000	TOTAL CURR LIABILITIES		229,000
LAND/BLDG	50,000		MORTGAGE	25,000	
EQUIP/FIX	50,000				
TOTAL FIXED ASSETS		100,000	TOTAL LONG TERM DEBT		25,000
			NET WORTH		143,000
TOTAL CA AND FA		$397,000	TOTAL LIAB AND NW		$397,000

PROFIT AND LOSS STATEMENT

NET SALES (LESS ALLOW & DISCOUNTS)	$700,000
COST OF GOODS SOLD	500,000
GROSS PROFIT	200,000

EXPENSES

DRAWINGS (OWNER)	$ 74,000
WAGES	65,000
DELIVERY	7,000
BAD DEBT	4,000
TELEPHONE	2,000
DEPRECIATION	4,000
INSURANCE	7,000
TAXES (LOCAL)	8,000
INTEREST	8,700
ADVERTISING	3,000
MISCELLANEOUS	2,000
TOTAL EXPENSES	$184,700

NET PROFIT (BEFORE FEDERAL TAXES) $ 15,300

RATIO: FIXED ASSETS TO NET WORTH

$$\frac{\text{FIXED ASSETS}}{\text{NET WORTH}} \quad \frac{100,000}{143,000} = 70\%$$

FIXED ASSETS TO
NET WORTH RATIO

MEASURES: The amount of fixed assets that are a part of net worth. This ratio is important because it provides an indication of how much capital is tied up in low-liquid assets.

GENERALLY ACCEPTED STANDARD: A rule of thumb for small business is that not more than 75% of your net worth should be tied up in fixed assets. If fixed assets are approaching 75% of the firm's net worth, the firm may be hurting for working capital to meet current expenses.

LOW RATIO: A proportionately smaller investment is fixed assets in relation to net worth, that is, net worth may consist of more liquid-type assets. This is a better situation for the creditors.

HIGH RATIO: A larger investment in plant and property, which may be hard to liquidate if cash is needed, especially if they are not paid for.

REMARKS: Fixed assets should be carried on the balance sheet as depreciated fixed assets, not original cost. The presence of substantial leased fixed assets (those not shown on a balance sheet) may deceptively lower this ratio. The amount of fixed assets depends on the industry: for example, the fixed asset requirement for a trucking company or a heavy equipment operating business may be relatively high, but it will be low for an average retailer or consultant and not too meaningful.

XYZ HARDWARE AND BUILDING SUPPLY
BALANCE SHEET
YEAR END 19XX

ASSETS			LIABILITIES		
CASH	$ 2,000		NOTES PAYABLE	$ 18,000	
ACCTS REC	85,000		ACCTS PAYABLE	205,000	
INVENTORY	210,000		ACCRUALS	6,000	
TOTAL CURR ASSETS		297,000	TOTAL CURR LIABILITIES		229,000
LAND/BLDG	50,000		MORTGAGE	25,000	
EQUIP/FIX	50,000				
TOTAL FIXED ASSETS		100,000	TOTAL LONG TERM DEBT		25,000
			NET WORTH		143,000
TOTAL CA AND FA		$397,000	TOTAL LIAB AND NW		$397,000

PROFIT AND LOSS STATEMENT

NET SALES (LESS ALLOW & DISCOUNTS)		$700,000
COST OF GOODS SOLD		500,000
GROSS PROFIT		200,000

EXPENSES

DRAWINGS (OWNER)	$ 74,000
WAGES	65,000
DELIVERY	7,000
BAD DEBT	4,000
TELEPHONE	2,000
DEPRECIATION	4,000
INSURANCE	7,000
TAXES (LOCAL)	8,000
INTEREST	8,700
ADVERTISING	3,000
MISCELLANEOUS	2,000
TOTAL EXPENSES	$184,700

NET PROFIT (BEFORE FEDERAL TAXES) $ 15,300

RATIO: INVESTMENT TURNOVER

$$\frac{\text{NET SALES}}{\text{TOTAL ASSETS}} \quad \frac{700,000}{397,000} \quad = \quad 1.8 \text{ Times}$$

INVESTMENT TURNOVER RATIO

MEASURES: Ability of the firm to generate sales in relation to assets.

GENERALLY ACCEPTED STANDARD: This will vary greatly depending on the business and the industry; for instance a service business would have limited fixed assets and little if any inventory compared to a manufacturing company.

LOW RATIO: The assets may not be fully employed or too many assets may be chasing too few sales. The assets are not pulling their own weight. The firm may be expanding but the business is not growing.

HIGH RATIO: More sales may be generated with fewer assets. This may indicate that something good is happening or has happened. Maybe you are getting more sales from the same level of buildings and equipment.

REMARKS: This ratio should be used only to compare firms within specific industry groups and in conjunction with other ratios. As with any ratio measuring assets, it can give a distorted reading if the assets are heavily depreciated or if there is a large amount of intangible assets, such as goodwill. Be careful when comparing two firms or comparing with the industry averages that the asset figures are approximately the same. This ratio does not consider a price increase or decrease or how well you watch your expenses. This ratio, when combined with the net profit ratio on page 36, becomes another return on investment (ROI) ratio. See page 40.

Another version is: $\dfrac{\text{Net Sales}}{\textbf{Fixed Assets}} = \dfrac{700,000}{100,000} = 7 \text{ Times}$

This is important if your business requires a large investment in fixed assets.

SUMMARY OF EFFICIENCY RATIOS

- Efficiency ratios measure how well you are conducting your business.

- Efficiency ratios help keep your business in balance.

- Your accounts receivable, times 365 days, divided by our credit sales will tell you the length of time it takes for your average customer to pay his/her bills.

- Dividing the cost of goods sold, by your average inventory, will provide you with the number of times you replace your inventory per month or per year.

- To find out the amount of fixed assets that are a part of your net worth-divide your fixed assets by your net worth.

- Your net sales divided by your total assets will tell you how well you are generating sales in relation to your total assets.

- A variation of the above ratio is to substitute fixed assets for total assets to see how well you are generating sales in relation to your fixed assets.

PART 4

HOW TO PERFORM A RATIO ANALYSIS

$$\frac{NET\ PROFIT}{NET\ WORTH} = ROI$$

RM

INTRODUCTION

Now that you have learned what ratios are and what they can do for you, we are ready to learn how to organize and use ratios analyzing a business. This section will provide forms and charts that will help you collect, organize, and evaluate your business through the use of a ratio review chart.

Data collection charts

The two forms on pages 60 and 61 will help you organize your ratios and assist you in using your **RATIO REVIEW CHART.** The first form is the **DATA GATHERING FORM.** It provides a means of gathering the necessary figures from the balance sheet and profit and loss statement.

The second form is the **COMPARISON CHART.** It provides spaces to work your ratios and insert your industry averages. Industry average figures are compiled by several sources. Some names and addresses of where to find industry average data are listed in the Appendix. This information may be purchased, but it is usually available through a banker, library, small business association office, or Chamber of Commerce. Your trade association may also compile similar statistics both nationally and regionally. Regional numbers may be more appropriate for your use. To make the best use of these forms, make several copies and use them by filling in the blanks from your balance sheet and profit and loss statement. Examples of filled in forms are shown on pages 58 and 59. These samples are based on the same balance sheet and profit and loss statement we have been using.

> The industry average ratios shown on the comparison chart, page 59, are taken from the 1987 Annual Statement Studies, asset size 0-1MM RETAILERS-BUILDING MATERIALS SIC# 5211, copyright by Robert Morris Associates, used with permission. Please note the disclaimer and other information in the Appendix.

WHAT IS SIGNIFICANT?

To determine which ratios to use, consider the type of business you have, the age of your business, the point in the business cycle, and what you are looking for. For instance, one type of business might require a large number of fixed assets, buildings, land, equipment, tools, etc. while another requires very few. The significant ratios in the first case would be those that help you measure how well you are using your fixed assets.

Another type of business may need to carry a well-stocked inventory or perhaps just enough to satisfy emergency needs. In either case, inventory turnover is critical, and if it gets out of hand, you may not be able to pay current expenses on the one hand, or have the stock to satisfy your customers on the other.

The age of your business is important. If you have passed the initial three to five years start-up period and have liquidity, you are probably interested in expansion. In this case, the profitability and efficiency ratios will be factors you need to closely monitor. Be careful to keep your business operations in balance.

Some businesses are dependent upon seasonality for their income. That is, more sales occur during certain periods of the year than any other. During each rise and fall of this cycle, ratios can be quite different. It becomes necessary to watch these periods so your ratios reflect what is needed. For example, if you are expecting a big sale, but it hasn't come through, or anticipating a low sales period, you will need liquidity to carry you through. If you sell on credit, you will need to watch your collection time between the sale and the payment, or you will face a lack of working capital.

Finally, if you are planning for expansion, you should be able to show regular profits which are in line with your industry. A low debt structure will also help influence lenders to provide the money you need at a favorable interest rate.

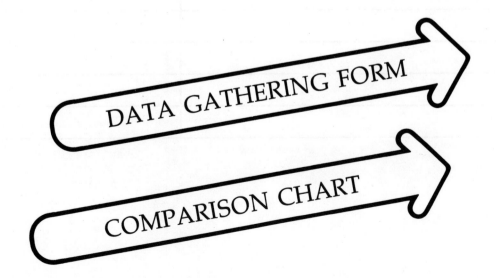

DATA GATHERING FORM

COMPARISON CHART

DATA GATHERING FORM

BUSINESS NAME: **XYZ Hardware and Building Supply**
BUSINESS ADDRESS: **Any Where U.S.A.**

DATE PREPARED: **DD/MM/YY**

ITEMS	DOLLAR FIGURES
CURRENT ASSETS	$ 297,000
CURRENT LIABILITIES	$ 229,000
NET SALES	$ 700,000
WORKING CAPITAL	$ 68,000
TOTAL DEBT	$ 254,000
NET WORTH	$ 143,000
EARNINGS BEFORE INTEREST AND TAXES	$ 24,000
NET PROFIT	$ 15,300
TOTAL ASSETS	$ 397,000
ACCOUNTS RECEIVABLE	$ 85,000
COST OF GOODS SOLD	$ 500,000
AVERAGE INVENTORY	$ 210,000
FIXED ASSETS	$ 100,000

COMPARISON CHART

BUSINESS NAME: **XYZ Hardware and Building Supply**
BUSINESS ADDRESS: **Any Where U.S.A.**

DATE PREPARED: **DD/MM/YY**

RATIO TITLE	RATIOS	DOLLAR FIGURES	MY RATIOS	INDUSTRY AVERAGES
CURRENT RATIO	CURRENT ASSETS / CURRENT LIABILITIES	$297,000 / $229,000	1.3 TIMES	2.0 TIMES
TURNOVER OF CASH	SALES / WORKING CAPITAL	$700,000 / $68,000	10.3 TIMES	8.1 TIMES
DEBT TO NET WORTH	TOTAL DEBT / NET WORTH	$254,000 / $143,000	1.8 TIMES	1.5 TIMES
NET PROFIT	EARNINGS BEFORE INT & TAXES / NET SALES	$24,000 / $700,000	3.4%	NOT LISTED*
RATE OF RETURN OF SALES	NET PROFIT** / NET SALES	$15,300 / $700,000	2.2%	3.2%
ROI	NET PROFIT** / NET WORTH	$15,300 / $143,000	10.7%	22.7%
ROA	NET PROFIT** / TOTAL ASSETS	$15,300 / $397,000	3.8%	8.9%
AVERAGE COLLECTION RATIO	ACCT'S REC'BLE × 365 / SALES	$85,000 × 365 / $700,000	44 DAYS	34.2** DAYS
INVENTORY TURNOVER	COST OF GOODS SOLD / AVERAGE INVENTORY	$500,000 / $210,000	2.4 TIMES	5.5 TIMES
FIXED ASSETS TO NET WORTH	FIXED ASSETS / NET WORTH	$100,000 / $143,000	70%	50%
INVESTMENT TURNOVER	NET SALES / TOTAL ASSETS	$700,000 / $397,000	1.8 TIMES	2.9 TIMES

** SEE THE APPENDIX

* Not all ratios are listed by all sources. The absence of one or two ratios should not significantly effect your analysis.

DATA GATHERING FORM

BUSINESS NAME: _____

BUSINESS ADDRESS: _____

DATE PREPARED: _____

ITEMS	DOLLAR FIGURES
CURRENT ASSETS	
CURRENT LIABILITIES	
NET SALES	
WORKING CAPITAL	
TOTAL DEBT	
NET WORTH	
EARNINGS BEFORE INTEREST AND TAXES	
NET PROFIT	
TOTAL ASSETS	
ACCOUNTS RECEIVABLE	
COST OF GOODS SOLD	
AVERAGE INVENTORY	
FIXED ASSETS	
TOTAL ASSETS	

(NOTE: This form may be copied by permission of the publisher)

COMPARISON CHART

BUSINESS NAME: _____

BUSINESS ADDRESS: _____

DATE PREPARED: _____

RATIO TITLE	RATIOS	DOLLAR FIGURES	MY RATIOS	INDUSTRY AVERAGES
CURRENT RATIO	CURRENT ASSETS / CURRENT LIABILITIES	_____		
TURNOVER OF CASH	SALES / WORKING CAPITAL	_____		
DEBT TO NET WORTH	TOTAL DEBT / NET WORTH	_____		
NET PROFIT	EARNINGS BEFORE INT & TAXES / NET SALES	_____		
RATE OF RETURN OF SALES	NET PROFIT / NET SALES	_____		
ROI	NET PROFIT / NET WORTH	_____		
ROA	NET PROFIT / TOTAL ASSETS	_____		
AVERAGE COLLECTION RATIO	ACCT'S REC'BLE × 365 / SALES	_____		
INVENTORY TURNOVER	COST OF GOODS SOLD / AVERAGE INVENTORY	_____		
FIXED ASSETS TO NET WORTH	FIXED ASSETS / NET WORTH	_____		
INVESTMENT TURNOVER	NET SALES / TOTAL ASSETS	_____		

(NOTE: This form may be copied by permission of the publisher)

RATIO REVIEW CHART

The chart on the next two pages provides a quick look at how your business is doing. You may discover things to check into because a ratio is too low. The page number for each ratio is listed to help refresh your memory of what each ratio means and how it is derived.

This review chart is more to help stimulate your thinking and not necessarily to provide answers. To make the best use of it make several copies and complete one each month with those ratios you feel are most important for your business. Please note that your industry averages are normally published quarterly so you may not have them for a month-to-month comparison. However, this chart can provide quick comparisons, and progress can be charted to help keep your business in balance.

Remember, things take time; don't try for too big a correction too quickly as such a move may cause problems in other areas.

"YOU TRY IT!"

RATIO REVIEW CHART

RATIO	YOUR RATIO	IND AVG*	IF MY RATIO IS HIGH	IF MY RATIO IS LOW
CURRENT ASSETS / CURRENT LIABILITIES (Pages 28-29)			Check your debt, savings accts, inventory, etc., to see that your money is working for you.	Check inventory, accts rec, and debt structure to see if you can obtain more cash.
SALES / WORKING CAPITAL (Pages 30-31)			Check the ratio above; see if you can obtain more cash.	You may have a cash surplus; invest it in the business, in savings, or pay debts.
TOTAL DEBT / NET WORTH (Pages 32-33)			Check your debt structure, both current and long term.	If too low, you should consider borrowing if the payback is right.
EBIT / NET SALES (Pages 36-37)			Generally, keep up the good work.	See below ratio for affect of interest/taxes.
NET PROFIT / NET SALES (Pages 38-39)			Generally, keep up the good work.	Check expenses and sales expectations.
NET PROFIT / NET WORTH (Pages 40-41)			Check your net worth structure, you could be undercapitalized or a good manager.	Check your debt structure, expenses or operating policies.
NET PROFIT / TOTAL ASSETS (Pages 42-43)			Generally, keep up the good work.	Check your operating policy for asset use.

(continued next page)

RATIO REVIEW CHART (Continued)

RATIO	YOUR RATIO	IND AVG*	IF MY RATIO IS HIGH	IF MY RATIO IS LOW
$\dfrac{\text{ACCTS REC} \times 365}{\text{SALES}}$ (Pages 46-47)			Check your credit policy.	Generally, keep up the good work.
$\dfrac{\text{COST OF GOODS SOLD}}{\text{AVERAGE INVENTORY}}$ (Pages 48-49)			Could be a good sign; check inventory and unfilled sales orders.	Check for over stocking or obsolete items; check cash flow.
$\dfrac{\text{FIXED ASSETS}}{\text{NET WORTH}}$ (Pages 50-51)			Check necessity of fixed assets.	Depends on your type of business.
$\dfrac{\text{NET SALES}}{\text{TOTAL ASSETS}}$ (Pages 52-53)			Generally, keep up the good work.	Check necessity for all assets; check if sales can't be increased.

*IND AVG = Industry Average

(This form may be copied by permission of the publisher)

> NOTE: These ratio charts do not take into account the age of a business, the time of the business cycle, local or national economic conditions, or any specific mixes of business. You should consider any one or more of these conditions at the time you are analyzing your business.

AFTERWORD

If One Ratio Goes Up Will Another Always Go Down?

Sometimes they do. But ratios generally don't work out so neatly.

Sometimes two or more ratios indicate good work and both will be high. Sometimes, depending on your type of business or the time in your business cycle, one will be low, or it won't make any difference what a ratio does.

Ratios are tools to help you analyze a business. In the next two parts of this book you will be introduced to other techniques that will help you keep your business in balance. It is important to remember that all tools will never be used all the time. If ratios are used improperly, it could worsen your position.

The proper use of ratios also takes into consideration the economy, the business cycle, and whether your business is just getting started, is achieving growth, or has reached maturity.

THINK IT THROUGH!

SUMMARY: HOW TO PERFORM A RATIO ANALYSIS

- The first step in determining the interaction between ratios is to record the proper dollar figures for the appropriate item (i.e. sales, net profit), from your balance sheet and profit and loss statement to the data gathering form.

- The second step is to transfer the dollar figures from the data gathering form to the comparison chart then determine your ratios and place them on the chart.

- The third step is to look up your industry ratio averages and place them on the comparison chart.

- The fourth step is to transfer your ratios and the industry averages to the ratio review chart and compare how your ratios match up with those of your industry. The ratio review chart will provide you a quick, cursory means of determining what corrective action you should take.

- The fifth step is to plan how to get those of yours that are off back on track .... and do it!

- All ratios will not be significant to you all the time.

- Ratios will react differently depending on your business' age, the time in the business cycle, the economic conditions, and your type of business.

PART 5

HOW TO PERFORM AN EXPENSE ANALYSIS

EXPENSE ANALYSIS

1. CREDIT
2. PAY OUTS
3. PAYROLL
4. INVENTORY
5. MARKETING
6. PURCHASING

IS ANYTHING GOOD ABOUT EXPENSES?

Expenses are a necessary part of doing business and should be treated as such. Expenses should not to be feared or denied. Expenses, however, must be taken into account when developing pricing policies, sales expectations, and a business plan.

Expenses are a fact of life for any business. But expenses that are too high will quickly ruin a business. This may seem obvious, but the point is, expenses must be controlled. The best way to do this is by understanding them; knowing what will result when you increase or decrease an expense.

Examining Your Expenses

Being familiar with and regularly examining your expenses, will help you every day that you are in business. Good expense control can help you maximize profits on the same or even fewer sales.

A good examination begins with the sales line on your P & L. By understanding why sales did or did not occur as projected, will put you in a better position to understand how the expenses of doing business behaved as they did. The first thing to note, is if a particular event happened that month, such as an unusually large sale. Perhaps what should have been a slow month suddenly became a strong one. Or vice-versa, perhaps bad weather caused shipments to be late and sales suffered. If you were unaware of factors affecting sales, you might overbuy inventory after an abnormal non-recurring sale. This could cause you to lose profits later on if you have to cut prices to move an aging inventory.

The Sales Line

Sales dollars or income is a function of unit price times unit volume. Therefore, an increase in either will increase sales dollars. Likewise, if either decreases (with no offsetting increase in the other parameter), sales dollars will drop. Marking down the price without an offsetting increase in volume will result in lower revenue and almost always a loss of profit. If you planned to take a trade discount to increase your inventory for a special sale and money wasn't available in time to take your discount, then when the merchandise arrived and the customers didn't, there would be double trouble.

EXAMINING YOUR EXPENSES
(Continued)

The Cost Of Goods Sold

The next item to evaluate while examining expenses is the cost of goods sold. Be sensitive to any increase or decrease as a percentage of net sales. Find causes for either an increase or decrease such as: purchased items that increased or decreased in price. Perhaps it is somethng like increased freight charges, spoilage, or shrinkage due to theft. This area often seems like a ''so what'' sort of category, but the success of many businesses can be determined by paying attention and sweating the details on the cost of goods sold line.

The cost of goods sold should be broken down into specific line items such as: freight in, manufacturing costs, discounts (taken or not taken) etc. A good review should include going through current invoices and comparing them with past invoices for the same merchandise to determine where the variances are and what caused them.

Credits And Collections

There is a cost in making money. The trick is to shorten the time between commitment of cash and the collection of cash. One of the best ways is to continually review expenses.

Fixed Expenses (Expenses whether or not a sale is made)

Let's move on to fixed expenses such as rent, interest, insurance, depreciation, taxes, and licenses. Each fixed expense should be spread in equal monthly installments for the year. If this is done, an increase in sales should cause profit margins to increase at a faster rate than if costs were variable (i.e., tied to sales). Fixed expenses can produce a greater return from increased sales than variable expenses. The reverse is also true if sales decrease and expenses are fixed and can't be reduced. Control of expenses, especially fixed expenses, should include the following:

1. Negotiate the best price for all products and services you purchase at the beginning. Use competitive bidding!
2. Try bartering.
3. Pay only as much and as often as you have to, continually look for better prices.
4. Never pay early.
5. Assume that all payment terms are negotiable.
6. Invest—don't spend.

EXAMINING YOUR EXPENSES
(Continued)

Variable Expenses (Tied to sales volume)

Variable expenses may include salaries, advertising costs, delivery, supplies, telephone, dues and subscriptions, and utilities. These costs should be analyzed in relation to their return on sales or other cost efficiencies. They are comparable with the "year to date" figures and percentages. These percentages should be in line with industry percentages and past experience. If sales rise or fall and action is not taken to adjust expenses, closer examination is necessary.

By carefully analyzing variable expenses you can determine their value in relation to creating sales or increasing margin. This is vital when forecasting, planning new product lines, or expansion, etc.

At the bottom of the statement is net profit.

Net profit may look okay, but there still may be trouble because of other variables. If some expense items were reduced and the profit margin did not rise, then something else occurred to offset the logical profit increase. There may be trouble in the cost of goods sold, for example. Remember that it's **collected dollars**, not *sales dollars* that you take to the bank. Don't confuse profits with cash flow.

WHAT TO DO WHEN THERE IS NO MORE ROOM TO CUT EXPENSES

When you run out of cost-cutting ideas, try increasing the return on your expenses. This can be done in several ways including:

1. **Examining your credit policy. Do you:**

   ☐ Invoice promptly?
   ☐ Provide clear information about your terms and collection policies?
   ☐ Maintain a receivables aging schedule and conduct a prompt follow-up on delinquent customers?
   ☐ Carefully check credit references?

2. **Examining your cash pay-outs. Do you:**

   ☐ Take advantage of trade discounts?
   ☐ Pay bills only when they are due?
   ☐ Try to establish extended terms with creditors to your advantage, such as expended dating or paying your debt over a long period of time?
   ☐ Buy only what is needed—when it is needed?

3. **Examining your payroll. Do you:**

   ☐ Before hiring a new employee consider: overtime? part-time help? temporary help? or free-lance workers?
   ☐ Pay all of your employees on the same day?
   ☐ Consider reducing your salary during slack periods and increasing it during better times?
   ☐ Check the amount of "downtime" caused by equipment or other controllable items?
   ☐ Check starting and quitting times?
   ☐ Check length of break times and personal times?
   ☐ Check petty cash flow?

4. **Examining your inventory controls. Do you:**

   ☐ Check your security to prevent theft?
   ☐ Instruct your employees about proper handling and storage to prevent breakage and damage to inventory?
   ☐ Calculate in the cost of inventory, the cost of storage, handling, insurance, taxes, deterioration, obsolescence, etc. to insure you aren't fooling yourself?
   ☐ Do you regularly check the turnover rate to see if your inventory can't be reduced.
   ☐ Look into just-in-time inventory, (i.e. keep your inventory levels to a logical minimum)?
   ☐ Always calculate a level of inventory relative to your needs?

WHAT TO DO WHEN THERE IS NO MORE ROOM TO CUT EXPENSES (Continued)

5. **Examining your manufacturing. Do you:**

   ☐ Get competitive bids from contractors?
   ☐ Look into contracting with smaller, less expensive "Cottage Suppliers."
   ☐ Tighten up planning and scheduling?
   ☐ Keep high quality standards? (Rework can be more costly.)

6. **Examining your marketing plan. Do you:**

   ☐ Avoid a "shotgun" approach to advertising and hope instead of targeting your specific customer group?
   ☐ Have a clear policy on returns and repairs?
   ☐ Make sure discounts are going to work, and have a way to end them if they don't?
   ☐ Train salespeople to sell accessory items?
   ☐ Demand quality courteous service for your customers?
   ☐ Train employees dealing directly with customers to maximize their positive initial impact?

7. **Examining your purchasing costs. Do you:**

   ☐ Control the items purchased to necessities?
   ☐ Insure all major purchases are competitively bid?
   ☐ Eliminate unprofitable products from your line?
   ☐ Look for more efficient ways to "build" your product?
   ☐ Maintain good working relationships with your vendors?

8. **Other areas to examine. Do you:**

   ☐ Use customer furnished material?
   ☐ Avoid early payment of expenses, (e.g. a year's supply of _____ ; or a three year payment of insurance, etc.?)
   ☐ Avoid unnecessary improvements?
   ☐ Avoid unnecessary volume purchases?
   ☐ Keep good records?
   ☐ Barter?
   ☐ Make cash deposits daily, investing surplus funds in interest bearing accounts?

SUMMARY OF HOW TO PERFORM AN EXPENSE ANALYSIS

- Expenses are a normal part of doing business and should be considered as such.

- Expenses can and should be controlled so you will know what you are getting for them.

- Begin your expense examination by analyzing sales.

- Next look at cost of goods sold. See if it has increased or decreased, and then find out why.

- Fixed expenses should not vary significantly with any increase or decrease in sales.

- Variable expenses may change with your sales volume.

- When you think you have cut expenses to the bone, there are eight major areas of your business you can examine to increase your return on expenses, (Pages 71-73)

PART 6

HOW TO CONTROL YOUR BUSINESS

HOW TO PROCEED

There are several ways to control your business. Some of the best ones involve financial analysis. This part of the book will bring together the use of ratios and percentages and present four basic techniques to help you control your business.

By control, we are talking not only about meeting industry averages, but about helping you forecast how much money it will take to prepare for a big promotional sale, or introduce a new product line or expand your sales. Control works two ways. First, it helps you improve what you are now doing and secondly it helps you prepare for expansion or change without being caught short of cash because you did not have a plan to keep things in balance.

The four techniques introduced in this part are:

1. Trend analysis
2. Cash position charting
3. Target statements
4. Accounts receivable aging schedule

We will consider each individually.

#1. Trend Analysis

The Data Gathering Form and the Comparison Chart which were introduced earlier will aid you in doing a trend analysis. A trend analysis is simply a method of keeping track of month to month and year to year ratios and expenses. It helps you stay on the right path by alerting you to adjustments you need to make to operate your business successfully.

Four charts found at the end of this section will help you do this. The first keeps track of your ratios month-to-month. The second is for tracking your year-to-year ratios. The third is for month-to-month expense tracking. And the forth is for tracking your year-to-year expenses.

HOW TO PROCEED (Continued)

Make a copy of each monthly chart at the beginning of your business year. Label each column with the appropriate name of the month. Record the month ending ratios or expenses in the proper column and you will soon have a monthly trend that you can study. Recording year end ratios and expenses on a yearly chart will build a yearly trend for you. The last column on the chart should list your goal or industry averages for each ratio or expense percent. This will allow you to chart how well you are progressing toward your goals.

By keeping track, you have a history of how well you are doing. These records are great for review and analysis and will help you plan future action.

The next two charts (pages 78 and 82) are examples of how you can use trends to better understand your business. In our first example, the ratio comparison chart provides a three year look at the XYZ Hardware and Building Supply Company. Our assumption is that the owner is trying to match or come close to the column labeled IND AVG (which stands for industry averages).

XYZ HARDWARE AND BUILDING SUPPLY
RATIO COMPARISON
THREE YEARS

RATIO	1ST YEAR	2ND YEAR	3RD YEAR	IND AVG
CURRENT ASSETS / CURRENT LIABILITIES	1.3 ×	1.9 ×	1.9 ×	2.0 ×
SALES / WORKING CAPITAL	10.3 ×	9.7 ×	8.8 ×	8.1 ×
TOTAL DEBT / NET WORTH	1.8 ×	1.5 ×	1.2 ×	1.5 ×
EBIT / NET SALES	3.4%	3.9%	4.0%	Not Listed*
NET PROFIT** / NET SALES	2.2%	2.4%	2.6%	3.2%
NET PROFIT** / NET WORTH	10.7%	14.7%	11.0%	22.7%
NET PROFIT** / TOTAL ASSETS	3.8%	4.0%	4.2%	8.9%
ACCT'S REC × 365 / SALES	44 Days	37.7 Days	46 Days	34.2 Days**
COST OF GOODS SOLD / AVERAGE INVENTORY	2.4 ×	3.7 ×	3.4 ×	5.5 ×
FIXED ASSETS / NET WORTH	70%	68.2%	64%	50%
NET SALES / TOTAL ASSETS	1.8 ×	1.6×	1.6×	2.9 ×

NOTE: × = Times; % = Percent; Days = average number of days it takes to collect credit sales; IND AVG = industry average. The industry average ratios shown are taken from the 1987 Annual Statement Studies, asset size 0-1MM, RETAILERS – BUILDERS MATERIALS, SIC# 5211, copyright by Robert Morris Associates, used with permission.

* Not all ratios are listed by all sources. The absence of one or two ratios should not significantly affect your analysis.

** Please note the disclaimer and other information in the appendix.

AUTHOR COMMENTS

XYZ Hardware and Building Supply Ratio Comparison Analysis

It appears that the current asset to liabilities ratio is moving in the right direction and that the sales to working capital is coming down. Total debt to net worth is below the industry average but still not at the 80% or below recommended figure. The earnings are almost there, and the profit to sales ratios is exceeding the average. The return on investment, however, rose, then fell, and is short of the average.

If the owner wished to get net profit up to the 22.7% average, he or she could increase sales and/or decrease expenses. Continuing on, the net profit to total assets is also rising, but is still not close to the average. Collection of credit sales were moving in the right direction, then slipped. Perhaps the owner extended the credit terms to increase sales. The inventory turnover did much the same, but dropped, which probably means that the company is still overstocked. The cash position hasn't changed much.

Fixed assets as a part of net worth is staying below the 75% level and dropping to the average of 50%. This may be due in part to the increase in working capital.

The turnover of sales to total assets is not moving toward the averages. This may be due to high inventory or more sales need to be generated for the amount of assets employed. This ratio should be run using fixed assets to see if they are in line.

So there is both good news and bad news for the XYZ Company but overall, progress is being made. As you review your trends you will want to check back to your original balance sheets and profit and loss statements, so be sure to save them. The next page summarizes the XYZ analysis and suggests actions to improve the business results.

AUTHOR RECOMMENDATIONS

Recommended actions to be taken by the XYZ Hardware and Building Supply Company include:

1. Reducing debt by replacing the inventory only when absolutely necessary. Apply the savings to pay off notes or the mortgage faster. The money gained from speeding up the collection of receivables can also be used to reduce debt. The reduction of debt should increase net worth because debt should decrease faster than current assets. The reduction of inventory and accounts receivable should help the net profit to total asset ratio.

2. Speeding up the collection of receivables will lower the average days' collection period. If credit terms were previously extended to increase sales, it doesn't appear to have helped. If this was done, credit terms need to be changed (i.e., tightened).

3. Slowing down stock purchasing. The inventory turnover ratio should improve.

4. Shrinking total assets should improve the sales to total assets ratio. However, increasing sales is a better way to do it.

Now let's see how expenses are measuring up.

EXPENSE ANALYSIS

AUTHOR COMMENTS

XYZ Hardware and Building Supply Expense Analysis:

The cost of goods sold ratio is holding steady and is close to the industry average, even as sales climb. Sales have increased each year by over 3%, but gross profit did not keep pace. This could be attributed to the owner not taking advantage of volume discounts or trade discounts or perhaps this is the nature of the business. The salary of the owner is roughly triple the industry average, which is part of the reason there is a lack of working capital. This may also be a contributing factor about why accounts payable is larger than it should be.

Employee salaries are coming in line with the industry average. This should be watched to insure the trend does not reverse itself.

Delivery expense is close to average, as is the bad debt figure. The drop in bad debt the third year may indicate better credit control and should be encouraged. Telephone and depreciation expenses are on target. Insurance payments seem high compared to the industry average and should be checked to see if the amount of coverage is really necessary. Meeting the industry average would add over $1,000 to profit. Taxes are also high and cost the company over $5,000 per year. Advertising is low but sales are rising. Sales may go up faster with more publicity. Net profit is falling in spite of rising sales, but beats the industry average, which shows a loss.

AUTHOR RECOMMENDATIONS

1. Check gross profit by investigating volume and/or trade discounts.

2. Keep up the good work on holding expenses.

3. Check into insurance payments and taxes to see if these items could be lowered.

4. And keep a eye on employee expenses as sales rise.

XYZ HARDWARE AND BUILDING SUPPLY
EXPENSE SHEET
THREE YEAR COMPARISON

EXPENSE ITEM	1ST YEAR		2ND YEAR		3RD YEAR		IND AVG
	$$ AM'T	%	$$ AM'T	%	$$ AM'T	%	%
SALES	700,000	100	725,000	100	750,000	100	100
COST OF G'DS SD	500,000	71	522,000	72	540,000	72	72.46
GROSS PROFIT	200,000	29	203,000	28	210,000	28	27.54
% INC IN SALES		3.4		3.3			
DRAWINGS (OWNER)	74,000	10.6	74,000	10.2	74,000	9.9	3.84
WAGES	65,000	9.3	65,000	9.0	75,000	10.0	10.43
DELIVERY	7,000	1.0	11,000	1.5	9,000	1.2	1.40
BAD DEBT	4,000	.6	4,000	.6	4,000	.5	.77
TELEPHONE	2,000	.3	2,000	.3	2,600	.3	.35
DEPRECIATION	4,000	.6	4,000	.6	4,000	.5	.58
INSURANCE	7,000	1.0	7,300	1.0	7,500	1.0	.80
TAXES (LOCAL)	8,000	1.1	8,000	1.1	8,000	1.1	.27
INTEREST	8,700	1.2	8,700	1.2	8,700	1.2	1.71
ADVERTISING	3,000	.4	4,000	.5	5,200	.7	.94
MISCELLANEOUS	2,000	.3	2,500	.3	4,000	.5	6.96 *
	$184,700	26.4	$190,500	26.3	$202,000	26.9	28.05
NET PROFIT	15,300	2.2	12,900	1.7	8,000	1.1	(.51)

NOTE: $$ AM'T = DOLLAR AMOUNT; IND AVG = industry average; COST OF G'DS SD = cost of goods sold; % INC IN SALES = percent increase in sales each year. Expense industry averages are from the 1982 Lumber/Building Materials Financial Report, copyright by the National Hardware Association, Indianapolis, IN. Used with permission.

*Miscellaneous includes donations, office and shop supplies, occupancy expense, credit card expense, leasing, legal and accounting, computer services, dues and subscriptions, entertainment, laundry, disposal, employee benefits, and other.

AUTHOR COMMENTS

A yearly example was used for this analysis, but it could have been monthly. In your analysis you should do both, since most businesses rise and fall substantially during a year's business cycle and comparing similar months year-by-year can be useful.

End-of-year figures are most commonly used to make trend charts. But if one particular month in your business cycle provides a more meaningful point in time, use that month as your starting point for yearly figures. Remember to start with the same month each time you prepare your yearly chart to make comparisons meaningful.

These numbers *must be coupled with honest experience and common sense to be of value.* A ratio consists of two figures. To change it you can raise one, lower the other, or do both. There is usually more than one choice. Before taking action, check (using target numbers) to see what effect your action may have on other ratios as some figures are used in more than one ratio. Following this page, there are the four blank forms (pages 84-87), which you may copy and use to analyze your trends.

NOTE: FORMS ON PAGES 84-87 MAY BE COPIED BY PERMISSION OF PUBLISHER

RATIO COMPARISON BY MONTH

BUSINESS NAME _____

BUSINESS ADDRESS _____

RATIO	MONTH						
CURRENT ASSETS / CURRENT LIABILITIES							
SALES / WORKING CAPITAL							
TOTAL DEBT / NET WORTH							
E-B-I-T / SALES							
NET PROFIT / NET SALES							
NET PROFIT / NET WORTH							
NET PROFIT / TOTAL ASSETS							
ACCT'S REC × 365 / SALES							
COST OF GOODS SOLD / AVERAGE INVENTORY							
FIXED ASSETS / NET WORTH							
NET SALES / TOTAL ASSETS							

RATIO COMPARISON BY YEAR

BUSINESS NAME _____

BUSINESS ADDRESS _____

RATIO	YEAR						
CURRENT ASSETS / CURRENT LIABILITIES							
SALES / WORKING CAPITAL							
TOTAL DEBT / NET WORTH							
E-B-I-T / SALES							
NET PROFIT / NET SALES							
NET PROFIT / NET WORTH							
NET PROFIT / TOTAL ASSETS							
ACCT'S REC × 365 / SALES							
COST OF GOODS SOLD / AVERAGE INVENTORY							
FIXED ASSETS / NET WORTH							
NET SALES / TOTAL ASSETS							

EXPENSE COMPARISON BY MONTH

MY BUSINESS: _____

BUSINESS ADDRESS: _____

MONTH							
EXPENSE ITEM	$$ AM'T	%	$$ AM'T	%	$$ AM'T	%	IND AVG
SALES							
COST OF G'DS SD							
GROSS PROFIT							
% INC (DEC) IN SALES							
DRAWINGS (OWNER)							
WAGES							
DELIVERY							
BAD DEBT							
TELEPHONE							
DEPRECIATION							
INSURANCE							
TAXES (LOCAL)							
INTEREST							
ADVERTISING							
MISCELLANEOUS							
NET PROFIT BEFORE TAXES							

EXPENSE COMPARISON BY YEAR

MY BUSINESS: _____

BUSINESS ADDRESS: _____

YEARS							
EXPENSE ITEM	$$ AM'T	%	$$ AM'T	%	$$ AM'T	%	IND AVG
SALES							
COST OF G'DS SD							
GROSS PROFIT							
% INC (DEC) IN SALES							
DRAWINGS (OWNER)							
WAGES							
DELIVERY							
BAD DEBT							
TELEPHONE							
DEPRECIATION							
INSURANCE							
TAXES (LOCAL)							
INTEREST							
ADVERTISING							
MISCELLANEOUS							
NET PROFIT BEFORE TAXES							

#2 Cash Position Charting

If there is only one thing you remember from this book, make it this: *Never run out of cash!*

In a small business operation a lack of cash, even for a short time, can cause all of your work and planning to become worthless. A cash shortage is the one thing that is most difficult to overcome. If you can't pay your bills, your help, or yourself, you won't be in business very long *even if you are showing a paper profit!*

To help avoid this situation especially when planning to do something different (such as expanding your business or taking on a new product line), a cash position chart will be of immeasurable value. This chart will help you target when cash will be needed to pay bills. It will also help you determine where to obtain cash to support items like expansion, (such as speeding up receivables collection, increasing cash sales, or borrowing). The cash position chart deals *only* with cash—cash paid out and cash taken in. It helps identify those periods when borrowing must be considered. This allows you to make arrangements for the cash *before* you actually need it. Pre-planning works wonders when talking with bankers.

An estimated cash position chart should be made a year in advance. A second chart should be used to record actual cash income and outgo on a weekly or monthly basis. By keeping track of outflow and inflow of cash and comparing these actual figures to your estimates, your budgeting ability will greatly improve. You will have good documents to show if you need to seek new money. Another version would be to make two columns for each month, one would be for the estimate the other would be for the actual. This method has the advantage of checking the accuracy of your estimates on one chart. Both types of charts are shown at the end of this section. The cash position on page 90 shows estimates for the beginning month plus the next five months.

CASH POSITION CHART (Continued)

In making your cash position chart follow the example on the next page. In the first column list starting cash that you believe will be available at the **end** of the beginning month. In the example shown, it is $200. Next, list the cash sales at the end of the month ($3,550 in our example). Then list the cash received from previous sales ($550 in our example) in the beginning month. This provides a total cash-in of $4,100.

To determine cash-out, list what you believe your expenses will be. In the example the expenses are: $1,000 purchases, $600 rent, $2,050 wages, and $350 for miscellaneous expenses, for a total cash-out of $4,000. Next add total cash-in to the starting cash balance and then subtract the total cash-out to obtain the ending balance, which is $300 in the example.

The cash position is found by subtracting the total cash-out from the total cash-in, or $100. Here we are interested only in the amount of cash created or lost during the beginning month. A loss is shown with the dollar figure between ( ), i.e. as a loss of $25 would be shown as (25).

Take the ending balance and place it at the top of the chart as the first month's starting cash figure. In our example this is $300. Then record the end of the month totals for cash-in and cash-out. The ending balance comes from adding the starting cash, $ 300, to the cash-in, $3,450, for a balance of $3,750, and subtracting total cash-out from it (3,950) for an ending balance in the first month of a negative $200, shown as (200). The cash flow for the first month is cash-out subtracted from cash-in, or a negative $500, shown as (500).

The first month's ending balance becomes the second month's starting cash (a negative $200). After the second month's ending totals are written in, our example shows that the ending balance is a positive $100. In other words, cash position has changed to a positive $300 and stays positive, as the cash sales and credit collections increase and expenses remain stable.

In the second month the projected ending balance and cash position both become positive.

CASH POSITION CHART

ITEMS	MONTHS					
	BEGIN	1ST	2ND	3RD	4TH	5TH
STARTING CASH	200	300	(200)	100	400	600
CASH-IN						
CASH SALES	3,550	2,950	4,000	3,300	3,000	3,200
CASH RECEIVED	550	500	1,550	1,800	2,000	2,000
TOTAL CASH-IN	4,100	3,450	5,550	5,100	5,000	5,200
CASH-OUT						
PURCHASES	1,000	1,000	2,500	2,000	2,000	2,000
RENT	600	600	600	600	600	600
WAGES	2,050	2,050	2,050	2,050	2,050	2,050
MISCELLANEOUS	350	300	100	150	150	150
TOTAL CASH-OUT	4,000	3,950	5,250	4,800	4,800	4,800
ENDING BALANCE	300	(200)	100	400	600	1,000
CASH POSITION	100	(500)	300	300	200	400

Note: ( ) means a loss or negative cash position. Your chart will be much more detailed than this example, which was shortened to simplify the explanation.

The cash position chart can also be used for planning cash positions, the following two examples (pages 91 and 92) provide a brief demonstration. For instance, you might want to consider borrowing instead of running a negative ending balance in the second month. The example on the facing page shows what would happen if you borrowed $200 in the beginning month.

PLANNING CASH POSITIONS

PLANNING CASH POSITIONS

Let's look at the example below. By starting with cash of $400, and keeping everything else the same, we see that there is no negative ending balance. But note the cash position is the same as in the example on page 90. This is because the difference between our cash-in and cash-out did not change. We start recording a positive cash position at the end of the second month as before.

CASH POSITION CHART

ITEMS	BEGIN	1ST	2ND	3RD	4TH	5TH
			MONTHS			
STARTING CASH	400*	500	0	300	600	800
CASH-IN						
CASH SALES	3,550	2,950	4,000	3,300	3,000	3,200
CASH RECEIVED	550	500	1,550	1,800	2,000	2,000
TOTAL CASH-IN	4,100	3,450	5,550	5,100	5,000	5,200
CASH-OUT						
PURCHASES	1,000	1,000	2,500	2,000	2,000	2,000
RENT	600	600	600	600	600	600
WAGES	2,050	2,050	2,050	2,050	2,050	2,050
MISCELLANEOUS	350	300	100	150	150	150
TOTAL CASH-OUT	4,000	3,950	5,250	4,800	4,800	4,800
ENDING BALANCE	500	0	300	600	800	1,200
CHANGE IN CASH POSITION	100	(500)	300	300	200	400

Note: * Assumes $200 has been borrowed
( ) means a loss or negative cash position.
Your chart will be much more detailed than this example which was shortened to simplify the explanation.
Interest paid on the loan would be an expense each month until paid. In this example it was not shown.

PLANNING CASH POSITIONS (Continued)

If you didn't want to borrow but wanted a positive ending balance and cash position, you could collect your receivables faster, reduce expenses, or postpone other expenses such as hiring. To see what happens if we reduce purchasing by $500 in the first month and second month, study the example below. The ending balance stays positive. Cash flow breaks even in the first month and also stays positive. If purchases could be reduced (perhaps increased at a later date) there would not be a negative cash position and this action could keep your cash flow positive and your business healthy.

CASH POSITION CHART

			MONTHS			
ITEMS	BEGIN	1ST	2ND	3RD	4TH	5TH
STARTING CASH	200	300	300	1,100	1,400	1,600
CASH-IN						
CASH SALES	3,550	2,950	4,000	3,300	3,000	3,200
CASH RECEIVED	550	500	1,550	1,800	2,000	2,000
TOTAL CASH-IN	4,100	3,450	5,550	5,100	5,000	5,200
CASH-OUT						
PURCHASES	1,000	500	2,000	2,000	2,000	2,000
RENT	600	600	600	600	600	600
WAGES	2,050	2,050	2,050	2,050	2,050	2,050
MISCELLANEOUS	350	300	100	150	150	150
TOTAL CASH-OUT	4,000	3,450	4,750	4,800	4,800	4,800
ENDING BALANCE	300	300	1,100	1,400	1,600	2,000
CASH POSITION	100	0	800	300	200	400

> Note: ( ) means a loss or negative cash position.
> Your chart will be much more detailed than this example, which was shortened to simplify the explanation.

By using a cash position chart you can keep your business solvent and learn your lessons on paper (not the hard way).

Pages 93 and 94 contain cash position charts. Improve your cash position by using one of them. These may be copied by permission of the publisher.

CASH POSITION CHART

BUSINESS NAME _____

BUSINESS ADDRESS _____

	MONTH	MONTH	MONTH	MONTH	MONTH	MONTH
BEGINNING OF MONTH CASH ON HAND						
CASH IN BANK						
OTHER CASH						
TOTAL CASH						
INCOME DURING MONTH CASH SALES						
CREDIT SALES RECEIPTS						
INVESTMENT INCOME						
OTHER INCOME						
TOTAL INCOME						
EXPENSES DURING MONTH PURCHASES (INVENTORY)						
OWNERS DRAWINGS						
SALARIES						
TAXES (PAYROLL)						
REPAIR/MAINTENANCE						
SELLING EXPENSE						
TRANSPORTATION						
LOAN PAYMENT						
OFFICE SUPPLIES						
UTILITIES						
TELEPHONE						
DUES/SUBSCRIPTIONS						
DEPRECIATION						
ADVERTISING						
RENT						
TAXES						
INSURANCE						
LEGAL/ACCOUNTING						
OTHER						
TOTAL EXPENSES END OF MONTH						
END OF MONTH BALANCE (LOSS)						
CHANGE IN CASH POSITION MONTHLY						

CASH POSITION CHART

BUSINESS NAME _____

BUSINESS ADDRESS _____

	MONTH		MONTH		MONTH	
	BUDGET	ACTUAL	BUDGET	ACTUAL	BUDGET	ACTUAL
BEGINNING OF MONTH CASH ON HAND						
CASH IN BANK						
OTHER CASH						
TOTAL CASH						
INCOME DURING MONTH CASH SALES						
CREDIT SALES RECEIPTS						
INVESTMENT INCOME						
OTHER INCOME						
TOTAL INCOME						
EXPENSES DURING MONTH PURCHASES (INVENTORY)						
OWNERS DRAWINGS						
SALARIES						
TAXES (PAYROLL)						
REPAIR/MAINTENANCE						
SELLING EXPENSE						
TRANSPORTATION						
LOAN PAYMENT						
OFFICE SUPPLIES						
UTILITIES						
TELEPHONE						
DUES/SUBSCRIPTIONS						
DEPRECIATION						
ADVERTISING						
RENT						
TAXES						
INSURANCE						
LEGAL/ACCOUNTING						
OTHER						
TOTAL EXPENSES END OF MONTH						
END OF MONTH BALANCE (LOSS)						
CHANGE IN CASH POSITION MONTHLY						

#3. Development of A Target Statement

A target statement is sometimes called a pro-forma statement. It is a model (or ideal) of the balance sheet and profit and loss statement. It is ideal because it is one that you wish to achieve. To make a target statement, begin by comparing your balance sheet and profit and loss statement percentages with those of your industry *or* those you wish to achieve.

Shown on pages 97 and 98 is a sample of a balance sheet and profit and loss statement of the XYZ Hardware and Building Supply Company which includes the percentages of all figures. Also listed is the target statement. In the example shown, the percentages of the industry are marked as industry averages (IA). The balance sheet percentages are percentages of the totals of the asset and liabilities columns respectively, shown as CA & FA (total current assets and fixed assets) and LIAB & NW (total liabilities and net worth). The profit and loss statement shows percentage of net sales. Let's assume that the owner wants to compare his or her averages to those of the industry.

Of course, any target could be used instead of the industry averages. From the example, notice that cash and inventory percentages are way out of line. The owner needs to reduce inventory to gain more cash. Note that the total current asset percentages are very close. The difference is in the mix of current assets.

On the liability side, the owner's bills, shown as accounts payable (ACCTS PAY), haven't been paid in a timely manner as is indicated by the big difference in percents between the statement percentages and the industry average percents. This is probably due to a lack of cash flow or positive cash position.

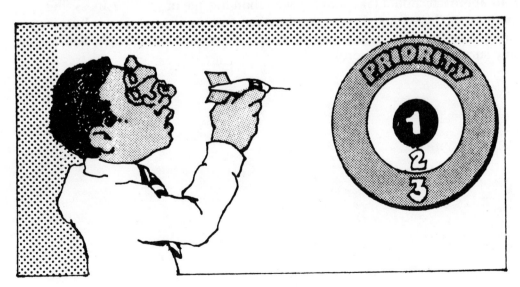

DEVELOPMENT OF A TARGET STATEMENT
(Continued)

The profit and loss statement also needs adjustment. The cost of goods sold is a little out of line. Perhaps this is because of the owner's inability to take trade or volume discounts, or possibly he or she is purchasing goods from a high cost vendor. The expenses could also use realignment. For instance, the advertising expense is very low. If increased, it might help promote greater sales, which in turn would lower the inventory and eventually gain some much needed cash. Also the owner's salary is too high for the current circumstances.

Once targets are selected, trying different combinations of sales, expenses, etc. should allow you to see what is required to achieve the financial position that is your goal.

Remember that reality-based experience must be used in making target statements. For instance, you probably won't jump 50% in sales or reduce expenses by half overnight. Don't expect instant results when experience tells you this won't happen. Steady progress toward your goal is the anwer. Balance your approach. You can't sacrifice one element very long without causing more problems somewhere else.

Develop your own target statement by using your balance sheets and profit and loss statements. Place a column on both reports, one for your averages and another column for your targets. Then compare the two. Determine the figures you need to meet your targets for each line item.

The use of ratios and a cash position chart will help you develop your strategy. Your approach should take into consideration the age of your business, the condition of the economy, your competition, and the nature of your business. Things take time, but if you keep your business finances in balance, you will not only survive, you should prosper.

XYZ HARDWARE AND BUILDING SUPPLY
BALANCE SHEET
YEAR END 19XX

ASSETS		%	IA%*	LIABILITIES		%	IA%*
CASH	$ 2,000	.5	7.7	NOTES PAY	$ 18,000	4.5	9.7
ACCTS REC	85,000	21.4	27.5	ACCTS PAY	205,000	51.7	17.7
INVENTORY	210,000	52.9	37.2	ACCRUALS	6,000	1.5	
TOTAL CA	297,000	74.8	74.4	TOTAL CL	229,000	57.7	39.1
LAND/BLDG	50,000			MORTGAGE	25,000		
EQUIP/FIX	50,000						
TOTAL FA	100,000	25.2	25.6	TOTAL LTD	25,000	6.3	17.8
				NET WORTH	143,000	36.0	40.7
CA & FA	$397,000	100.0	100.0	LIAB & NW	$397,000	100.0	100.0

* IA% = INDUSTRY AVERAGES. These percentages are taken from the 1987 Annual Statement Studies, asset size 0-1MM, RETAILERS-BUILDING MATERIAL SIC #5211, copyright by Robert Morris Associates, used with permission. Please note the disclaimer and other information in the appendix.

EXPLANATION OF THE CONTENTS INCLUDED IN THE INDUSTRY AVERAGES
INCLUDED IN TOTAL CA ARE 2.0% OF ALL OTHER CURRENT ASSETS.

INCLUDED IN TOTAL FA ARE .3% INTANGIBLES AND 4.5% OF ALL OTHER NON-CURRENT.

INCLUDED IN TOTAL CL ARE CURRENT MATURING LTD. 3.4%, INCOME TAX PAYABLES .8%, AND ALL OTHER CURRENT 7.6%.

INCLUDED IN LIAB AND NW ARE DEFERRED TAXES .5% AND OTHER NON-CURRENT 1.9%.

XYZ HARDWARE AND BUILDING SUPPLY
PROFIT AND LOSS STATEMENT
FOR THE YEAR OF 19____

				%	IA%**
NET SALES (LESS ALLOW & DISCOUNTS)			$700,000	100.0	100.00
COST OF GOODS SOLD			500,000	71.4	72.46
GROSS PROFIT			200,000	28.6	27.54
EXPENSES		%	IA%**		
DRAWINGS (OWNER)	$ 74,000	10.6	3.84		
WAGES	65,000	9.3	10.43		
DELIVERY	7,000	1.0	1.40		
BAD DEBT	4,000	.6	.77		
TELEPHONE	2,000	.3	.35		
DEPRECIATION	4,000	.6	.58		
INSURANCE	7,000	1.0	.80		
TAXES (LOCAL)	8,000	1.1	.27		
INTEREST	8,700	1.2	1.71		
ADVERTISING	3,000	.4	.94		
MISCELLANEOUS	2,000	.3	6.96*		
TOTAL EXPENSES	184,700	26.4	28.5		

		%	IA%**
NET PROFIT (BEFORE FEDERAL TAXES)	$15,300	2.2	(.51)

**Expense industry averages are from the 1982 Lumber/Building Materials Financial Report, copyright by the National Hardware Association, Indianapolis, IN, used with permission.

*Miscellaneous includes donations, office and shop supplies, occupancy expense, credit card expense, leasing, legal and accounting, computer services, dues and subscriptions, entertainment, laundry, disposal, employee benefits, and other.

#4 Accounts Receivable Aging Schedule

The accounts receivable aging schedule is a control technique that can save you both money and headaches. It is a simple tool. Just keep a record, as shown on page 100, as a reminder of customers who still owe you. A timely follow up, with an appropriate overdue notice to delinquent customers, can head off an account that may be "forgotten" forever.

The table below provides an indication that the longer you wait to collect your accounts receivable, the less likely you are to receive full payment.

This table of collection likelihood for accounts receivable assumes that you have the correct information concerning the address for a customer or the address and a credit check for a business buying finished goods or raw material.

PAST DUE BY:	PROBABILITY OF COLLECTION
30 DAYS	95 PERCENT
60 DAYS	82 PERCENT
120 DAYS	70 PERCENT
6 MONTHS	49.5 PERCENT

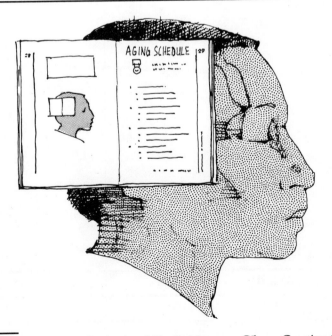

*Reported by John W. Rogers, Professional Credit Manager, Gibson Greeting Cards, Cincinnati, Ohio. Used with permission.

ACCOUNTS RECEIVABLE AGING SCHEDULE
XYZ HARDWARE AND BUILDING SUPPLY

		ACCOUNTS RECEIVABLE AGING SCHEDULE			
			PAST DUE BY		
CUSTOMER	TOTAL	CURRENT	30-59 DAYS	60-119 DAYS	120-180 DAYS
A	5,000	3,000	2,000		
B	2,000	1,000		1,000	
C	1,000	1,000			
D	4,000	1,000		3,000	
E	3,000	1,000	500	500	1,000
F	12,000	10,000	2,000		
G	3,000	2,000		1,000	
H	5,000	3,000	1,000	1,000	
I	3,000	3,000			
J	2,000	2,000			
K	10,000	10,000			
L	3,000	2,000			1,000
M	7,000	5,000		2,000	
N	2,000	2,000			
O	8,000	7,000	1,000		
P	6,000	3,000	3,000		
Q	6,000		500	4,500	1,000
R	3,000			1,000	2,000
TOTAL	85,000	56,000	10,000	14,000	5,000
PRECENT	100%	66%	12%	16%	6%

NOTE: Days refers to calendar days not working days.

SUMMARY OF HOW TO CONTROL YOUR BUSINESS

CHECK THOSE THAT YOU INTEND TO USE:

☐ A trend analysis is an excellent technique to help me measure the direction my business is going.

☐ A month-by-month and year-by-year comparison will accurately develop the trend my business is taking.

☐ I plan never to run out of cash.

☐ Cash position charting will help me forecast when and how much money I will need to carry out plans.

☐ A target statement is the development of a balance sheet and a profit and loss statement as a "target" which I wish to hit.

☐ The accounts receivable aging schedule is a must if I do credit business.

☐ The accounts receivable aging schedule will help remind me of accounts that are past due and require special attention.

blank page 102

APPENDIX

Listed below are several sources for locating your industry ratios and expense percentages. This is not an exhaustive list. Your local or university library, trade association, or Chamber of Commerce may be of further assistance.

DUNN AND BRADSTREET, INC.
PUBLIC RELATIONS DEPARTMENT
99 CHURCH STREET
NEW YORK, NY 10007
> Includes 22 retail; 32 wholesale; 71 industrial businesses called ''key business ratios.'' Also ''Cost of Doing Business,'' includes operating ratios.

ROBERT MORRIS ASSOCIATES
PHILADELPHIA NATIONAL BANK BUILDING
PHILADELPHIA, PA 10107
> Includes 350 lines of business.

ACCOUNTING CORPORATION
RESEARCH DEPARTMENT
1929 FIRST AVENUE
SAN DIEGO, CA 92101
> Publishes semiannually the (MAIL-ME-MONDAY) barometer of small business. Classifies operating ratios for various industry groups. The emphasis is on small business.

THE SMALL BUSINESS REPORTER
DEPARTMENT 3120
P.O. BOX 37000
SAN FRANCISCO, CA
> Provided by the Bank of America. It includes problems in opening a small business.

NATIONAL CASH REGISTER COMPANY
DAYTON, OHIO 45479
> Examines about 40 lines of business. With emphasis on expenses.

Interpretation of Statement Studies Figures[1]

RMA recommends that Statement Studies data be regarded only as general guidelines and not as absolute industry norms. There are several reasons why the data may not be fully representative of a given industry:

1. The financial statements used in the *Statement Studies* are not selected by any random or statistically reliable method. RMA member banks voluntarily submit the raw data they have available each year, with these being the only constraints: (a) The fiscal year-ends of the companies reported may not be from April 1 through June 29, and (b) their total assets must be less than $100 million.
2. Many companies have varied product lines; however, the *Statement Studies* categorize them by their primary product Standard Industrial Classification (SIC) number only.
3. Some of our industry samples are rather small in relation to the total number of firms in a given industry. A relatively small sample can increase the chances that some of our composites do not fully represent an industry.
4. There is the chance that an extreme statement can be present in a sample, causing a disproportionate influence on the industry composite. This is particularly true in a relatively small sample.
5. Companies within the same industry may differ in their method of operations, which in turn can directly influence their financial statements. Since they are included in our sample, too, these statements can significantly affect our composite calculations.
6. Other considerations that can result in variations among different companies engaged in the same general line of business are different labor markets; geographical location; different accounting methods; quality of products handled; sources and methods of financing; and terms of sale.

For these reasons, RMA does not recommend the Statement Studies *figures be considered as absolute norms for a given industry. Rather the figures should be used only as general guidelines and in addition to the other methods of financial analysis. RMA makes no claim as to the representativeness of the figures printed in this book.*

**Net profit is net profit before federal taxes in all ratios.

34.2 days is not a direct quote from Robert Morris Associates. It was developed by the author by multiplying the TRADE RECEIVABLES (27.5%) TIMES TOTAL ASSETS ($98,770) = $27,161.75 to obtain the acc'ts rec'ble; TIMES 365 DAYS PER YEAR = 9,914,038.80; DIVIDED BY NET SALES OF $289,838.00 = 34.2 days outstanding.

The above information is on page 261 of the 1987 annual statement studies, asset size 0-1MM, retailers-building materials, SIC #5211.

---

[1] ©1987 by Robert Morris Associates

NOTES

FOR OTHER FIFTY-MINUTE SELF-STUDY BOOKS
SEE ORDER FORM AT THE BACK OF THE BOOK.

NOTES

FOR OTHER FIFTY-MINUTE SELF-STUDY BOOKS
SEE ORDER FORM AT THE BACK OF THE BOOK.

NOTES

FOR OTHER FIFTY-MINUTE SELF-STUDY BOOKS
SEE ORDER FORM AT THE BACK OF THE BOOK.

NOTES

FOR OTHER FIFTY-MINUTE SELF-STUDY BOOKS
SEE ORDER FORM AT THE BACK OF THE BOOK.

NOTES

FOR OTHER FIFTY-MINUTE SELF-STUDY BOOKS
SEE ORDER FORM AT THE BACK OF THE BOOK.

NOTES

THE FIFTY-MINUTE SERIES

Quantity	Title	Code #	Price	Amount
	MANAGEMENT TRAINING			
	Self-Managing Teams	000-0	$7.95	
	Delegating For Results	008-6	$7.95	
	Successful Negotiation—Revised	09-2	$7.95	
	Increasing Employee Productivity	010-8	$7.95	
	Personal Performance Contracts—Revised	12-2	$7.95	
	Team Building—Revised	16-5	$7.95	
	Effective Meeting Skills	33-5	$7.95	
	An Honest Day's Work: Motivating Employees To Excel	39-4	$7.95	
	Managing Disagreement Constructively	41-6	$7.95	
	Training Managers To Train	43-2	$7.95	
	Learning To Lead	043-4	$7.95	
	The Fifty-Minute Supervisor—Revised	58-0	$7.95	
	Leadership Skills For Women	62-9	$7.95	
	Systematic Problem Solving & Decision Making	63-7	$7.95	
	Coaching & Counseling	68-8	$7.95	
	Ethics In Business	69-6	$7.95	
	Understanding Organizational Change	71-8	$7.95	
	Project Management	75-0	$7.95	
	Risk Taking	76-9	$7.95	
	Managing Organizational Change	80-7	$7.95	
	Working Together In A Multi-Cultural Organization	85-8	$7.95	
	Selecting And Working With Consultants	87-4	$7.95	
	PERSONNEL MANAGEMENT			
	Your First Thirty Days: A Professional Image in a New Job	003-5	$7.95	
	Office Management: A Guide To Productivity	005-1	$7.95	
	Men and Women: Partners at Work	009-4	$7.95	
	Effective Performance Appraisals—Revised	11-4	$7.95	
	Quality Interviewing—Revised	13-0	$7.95	
	Personal Counseling	14-9	$7.95	
	Attacking Absenteeism	042-6	$7.95	
	New Employee Orientation	46-7	$7.95	
	Professional Excellence For Secretaries	52-1	$7.95	
	Guide To Affirmative Action	54-8	$7.95	
	Writing A Human Resources Manual	70-X	$7.95	
	Winning at Human Relations	86-6	$7.95	
	WELLNESS			
	Mental Fitness	15-7	$7.95	
	Wellness in the Workplace	020-5	$7.95	
	Personal Wellness	021-3	$7.95	

THE FIFTY-MINUTE SERIES (Continued)

Quantity	Title	Code #	Price	Amount
	WELLNESS (CONTINUED)			
	Preventing Job Burnout	23-8	$7.95	
	Job Performance and Chemical Dependency	27-0	$7.95	
	Overcoming Anxiety	029-9	$7.95	
	Productivity at the Workstation	041-8	$7.95	
	COMMUNICATIONS			
	Technical Writing In The Corporate World	004-3	$7.95	
	Giving and Receiving Criticism	023-X	$7.95	
	Effective Presentation Skills	24-6	$7.95	
	Better Business Writing—Revised	25-4	$7.95	
	Business Etiquette And Professionalism	032-9	$7.95	
	The Business Of Listening	34-3	$7.95	
	Writing Fitness	35-1	$7.95	
	The Art Of Communicating	45-9	$7.95	
	Technical Presentation Skills	55-6	$7.95	
	Making Humor Work	61-0	$7.95	
	Visual Aids In Business	77-7	$7.95	
	Speed-Reading In Business	78-5	$7.95	
	Publicity Power	82-3	$7.95	
	Influencing Others	84-X	$7.95	
	SELF-MANAGEMENT			
	Attitude: Your Most Priceless Possession-Revised	011-6	$7.95	
	Personal Time Management	22-X	$7.95	
	Successful Self-Management	26-2	$7.95	
	Balancing Home And Career—Revised	035-3	$7.95	
	Developing Positive Assertiveness	38-6	$7.95	
	The Telephone And Time Management	53-X	$7.95	
	Memory Skills In Business	56-4	$7.95	
	Developing Self-Esteem	66-1	$7.95	
	Creativity In Business	67-X	$7.95	
	Managing Personal Change	74-2	$7.95	
	Stop Procrastinating: Get To Work!	88-2	$7.95	
	CUSTOMER SERVICE/SALES TRAINING			
	Sales Training Basics—Revised	02-5	$7.95	
	Restaurant Server's Guide—Revised	08-4	$7.95	
	Telephone Courtesy And Customer Service	18-1	$7.95	
	Effective Sales Management	031-0	$7.95	
	Professional Selling	42-4	$7.95	
	Customer Satisfaction	57-2	$7.95	
	Telemarketing Basics	60-2	$7.95	
	Calming Upset Customers	65-3	$7.95	
	Quality At Work	72-6	$7.95	
	Managing Quality Customer Service	83-1	$7.95	
	Quality Customer Service—Revised	95-5	$7.95	
	SMALL BUSINESS AND FINANCIAL PLANNING			
	Understanding Financial Statements	022-1	$7.95	
	Marketing Your Consulting Or Professional Services	40-8	$7.95	

THE FIFTY-MINUTE SERIES (Continued)

Quantity	Title	Code #	Price	Amount
	SMALL BUSINESS AND FINANCIAL PLANNING (CONTINUED)			
	Starting Your New Business	44-0	$7.95	
	Personal Financial Fitness—Revised	89-0	$7.95	
	Financial Planning With Employee Benefits	90-4	$7.95	
	BASIC LEARNING SKILLS			
	Returning To Learning: Getting Your G.E.D.	002-7	$7.95	
	Study Skills Strategies—Revised	05-X	$7.95	
	The College Experience	007-8	$7.95	
	Basic Business Math	024-8	$7.95	
	Becoming An Effective Tutor	028-0	$7.95	
	CAREER PLANNING			
	Career Discovery	07-6	$7.95	
	Effective Networking	030-2	$7.95	
	Preparing for Your Interview	033-7	$7.95	
	Plan B: Protecting Your Career	48-3	$7.95	
	I Got the Job!	59-9	$7.95	
	RETIREMENT			
	Personal Financial Fitness—Revised	89-0	$7.95	
	Financial Planning With Employee Benefits	90-4	$7.95	

OTHER CRISP INC. BOOKS

Quantity	Title	Code #	Price	Amount
	Desktop Publishing	001-9	$ 5.95	
	Stepping Up To Supervisor	11-8	$13.95	
	The Unfinished Business Of Living: Helping Aging Parents	19-X	$12.95	
	Managing Performance	23-7	$19.95	
	Be True To Your Future: A Guide To Life Planning	47-5	$13.95	
	Up Your Productivity	49-1	$10.95	
	Comfort Zones: Planning Your Future 2/e	73-4	$13.95	
	Copyediting 2/e	94-7	$18.95	
	Recharge Your Career	027-2	$12.95	
	Practical Time Management	275-4	$13.95	

VIDEO TITLE*

Quantity	Video Title*	Code #	Preview	Purchase	Amount
	Attitude: Your Most Priceless Possession	012-4	$25.00	$395.00	
	Quality Customer Service	013-2	$25.00	$395.00	
	Team Building	014-2	$25.00	$395.00	
	Job Performance & Chemical Dependency	015-9	$25.00	$395.00	
	Better Business Writing	016-7	$25.00	$395.00	
	Comfort Zones	025-6	$25.00	$395.00	
	Creativity in Business	036-1	$25.00	$395.00	
	Motivating at Work	037-X	$25.00	$395.00	
	Calming Upset Customers	040-X	$25.00	$395.00	
	Balancing Home and Career	048-5	$25.00	$395.00	
	Stress and Mental Fitness	049-3	$25.00	$395.00	

(*Note: All tapes are VHS format. Video package includes five books and a Leader's Guide.)

	Amount
Total Books	
Less Discount (5 or more different books 20% sampler)	
Total Videos	
Less Discount (purchase of 3 or more videos earn 20%)	
Shipping ($3.50 per video, $.50 per book)	
California Tax (California residents add 7%)	
TOTAL	

☐ Send volume discount information.   ☐ Please send me a catalog.

☐ Please charge the following credit card   ☐ Mastercard   ☐ VISA   ☐ AMEX

Account No. _____   Name (as appears on card) _____

Ship to: _____   Bill to: _____

_____   _____

_____   _____

_____   _____

Phone number: _____   P.O. # _____

All orders except those with a P.O.# must be prepaid.
For more information Call (415) 949-4888 or FAX (415) 949-1610.

‖‖‖‖